CHAPTERS

CHAPTERS

Create a Life of Exhilaration and
Accomplishment in the Face of Change

Candice Carpenter

McGraw-Hill

New York   Chicago   San Francisco   Lisbon   London
Madrid   Mexico City   Milan   New Delhi
San Juan   Seoul   Singapore   Sydney   Toronto

Library of Congress Cataloging-in-Publication Data

Carpenter, Candice.
    Chapters : create a life of exhilaration and accomplishment in the face of change /
Candice Carpenter.
      p.   cm.
    ISBN 0-07-138181-3 (alk. paper)
    1. Success—Psychological aspects. 2. Change (Psychology). I. Title.

BF637. S8 C3755   2001
158.1—dc21   2001044009

McGraw-Hill

A Division of The McGraw-Hill Companies

This book was set in Electra by MM Design 2000, Inc.
Printed and bound by R. R. Donnelley & Sons Company.

McGraw-Hill books are available at special quantity discounts to use as premiums
and sales promotions, or for use in corporate training programs. For more information, please write to the Director of Special Sales, Professional Publishing, McGraw-
Hill, Two Penn Plaza, New York, NY 10121-2298. Or contact your local bookstore.

This book is printed on recycled, acid-free paper containing a minimum
of 50% recycled, de-inked fiber.

To my husband Peter Olson,
for making all of my dreams come true,
and my beautiful little girls, Michaela and Ellie—
I pray that your lives will be a constant unfolding of dreams
and contribution, and that I have given you a sense that this
is your planet to dance on and care for.

Contents

Who Should Read This Book

*T*his book is for employees who dream of other jobs, other places, other careers. It's for leaders who want to make their organizations as fluid as the world we live in today, or just ease the discomfort of those who look to them for help. For the young just starting out in the workplace, for women trying to balance the competing claims of jobs and families, for husbands and fathers who worry that their success is won at the cost of their children, this book has a simple message: You don't have to be all things at once, but you can be everything you want to be.

Whether you love your job or hate it, whether you long to live out a secret yearning or just want to get more comfortable with the ever-shifting terrain of modern life, this book gives you a new way to look at the world. *Chapters* isn't about coping with change, or surviving it. It's about learning to dance with change, about accepting risk and unlocking your own optimism and creativity. Instead of climbing a ladder toward an elusive sense of happiness, this book teaches you to live your life in waves, and it shows you why the spaces between your great accomplishments are every bit as important as the accomplishments themselves.

For those who have just lost their jobs or those who have fired themselves, this book provides a practical process of reinvention that will help you land in a better place than the one you just left. It also teaches you how to be a Navigator to those who are in transition—when to offer counsel and when to just be there for them. Even more important, it shows you what to look for in yourself: the warning signs that say it is time to go, the often silent signals that tell you where you are headed next. This book isn't just about doing well; it's about leaving well so you can find the Zone of pure involvement and happiness time and time again.

This is a book about bringing your dreams—all your dreams—and your reality into alignment. It's about harmonizing the cycles of your own life with the lives of those you love and using coupleship creatively so that both parties can find their own best selves, with less stress. You will learn in these pages how a series of work chapters can capture and express your desire to make a difference, raise terrific kids, acquire wealth, and leave a legacy to those who come behind you. *Chapters* is my guidebook to fashioning a life of exhilaration and accomplishment in the twenty-first century.

CANDICE CARPENTER

Acknowledgments

I would like to thank some of the pioneering thinkers and practitioners in this area, who were so generous with me as my passion and obsession with it grew—John O'Neil, Bill Bridges, Robert Fritz, and David Nadler. I would like to thank Donald Marrs for writing a book of such stunning honesty that it inspired me to his standard, and Yankelovich Partners and The Families and Work Institute for providing such an important overview of the state of our generational values and needs around work. Additional thanks go to Phil Simhauser, David Zelman, and Carole Hyatt for illustrating what I believe to be one of the new professions of our century— Navigators. And thanks also go to the very successful people who graciously shared the unvarnished version of their work journeys so we could all learn from them. I would like to thank my collaborator, Howard Means, for his poetry and commitment to this project; Al Lowman, who never seemed to doubt that this book could make an important contribution; and the people at McGraw-Hill, who made every aspect of this project such a pleasure. Finally, to Ted Leonsis, who is one of our generations great visionaries who brought many dreams to fruition.

CHAPTER ONE

At the Heart of All True Change

*The important thing is this: that we should be
able at any moment to sacrifice what we are for
what we could become.*

—**Charles DuBos**

*T*hanks to a diverse career that has taken me from a global financial services company and an international media conglomerate to, most recently, an Internet start-up backed by $250 million in venture and public market capital, I've been face-to-face with just about every major business trend of the last two decades. Whiplash or not, I wouldn't trade the ride, but it has taught me one lesson above all else: The changes shaping our professional lives are every bit as sweeping and ultimately more important than the changes impacting our companies.

Many of us have spent years mastering the principles of innovation on behalf of the companies and organizations we run or work for. We've learned to live with faster product cycles because we've had no choice. To assure that fresh blood is always flowing through the corporate brain, we've taken what once seemed radical concepts, such as "skunkworks" and "thinking outside the box," and turned them into standard operating procedure. Now we need to apply those same principles to ourselves, and to the quest for our own professional accomplishment and personal fulfillment.

> We've all become great innovators on behalf of our companies and our work environments. Now we need to turn that spirit of radical innovation to our own lives.

The acceleration of company and even industry cycles, the harsh realities of global competition, the sometimes insane pressure on short-term results—these aren't just business problems. Nor are the instability caused by dual-income families and the dislocation caused by what can seem an almost constant stream of closures, mergers, and acquisitions solely social problems. First and foremost, they are all human problems, whether the human involved is a CEO, a division head, or the new code writer fresh out of college. And it's in this humanware, not the software or the hardware, where the real questions simmer, where the real issues lie, and where the capacity for fluidity and reinvention finally makes the greatest difference. Simply put, at the heart of all true change are people.

I speak all over the country, and what I hear is longing, restlessness, and trauma from so much change and from dreams that won't stay in their cage. The restlessness, I think, explains the popularity of "change strategy" books. People are dying, sometimes almost literally, for anything to help them survive and prosper in this new world we all find ourselves inhabiting. The problem is that the books aren't quite giving people the answers they need. We can do more than simply react to the change that inundates us. We can learn to dance with it, to move to its waves and rhythms. Instead of drowning in change or just treading water to keep our head above its surface, we can make art of the churn. We can, and what's more, we must.

We humans love stasis. The best experts I've been able to find tell me that no more than one in ten of us finds dealing with change easy or natural. But stasis no longer loves us. All of us can expect to hold eight to ten jobs in our adult lifetime and to pursue three distinct careers. What does that mean? That adaptability will be as important as hard skills and that the choosing will be as important as the choice. Of the 67 factors that Leadership Architects, a Minnesota company that identifies future leaders for 800 corporate clients, includes in its predictive system for job success, only one is related to the mastery of specific skills. Others include aspiration, suitability, character fit, and above all—fluidity.

> We may love stasis, but stasis no longer loves us.

Most important, this multiplicity means that the spaces between the jobs and careers that make up our professional lives are going to be as important as the jobs themselves because it is in the spaces that we truly get to determine what kind of person we will become and what kind of trajectory we will set. Just as surely as the 1980s were about aggression and the 1990s about speed, the first decade of this new century, I'm convinced, is going to be about mastering the gaps in our lives. It's going to be about fluidity and about the courage to imagine life not as a constant but as a constant process of creation.

Because I was fortunate enough to have been an integral part of perhaps the most neurotically accelerated business cycle the world has ever seen, I had a chance to see close up the impact of change on my colleagues and employees — people I cared deeply for, caught in a whirlwind. From that experience, I learned one more thing: Whether we yet have the words for it or not, this fluidity, this capacity to dance with change, the courage to embrace movement instead of stasis, is what most of us today most deeply desire. Back in 1992 after he had created Fox, the first new television network in 30 years, my old boss and teacher Barry Diller set off across the country with his Powerbook to spend a year understanding the new landscape. Barry's search finally led him to the Internet, just as it was beginning to alter almost everything about the way we do business and live. As my obsession with change and its effect on our careers and lives has grown, I've been on a trek of my own these past 12 months, searching for answers to the questions that have been burning inside me.

If change is now as much a part of our work lives as 401(k)s and performance reviews, then how can we make ourselves its master and how will our lives look as that happens? How can we use our mastery of change to finally create a balance between work and families, and between our desire to acquire wealth and power and our desire to make a difference in the world? Indeed, can we get so skillful at this thing called change that we can make it work for us, to create the professional and personal lives we most desire at any point in time? These are the questions that truly matter, I've come to believe. These are the issues that will determine not just our professional success but our personal happiness, too. If we can learn to fit the rhythms of change in our own lives to the rhythms of change in our work lives and in life as a whole, then I believe we're in for one heck of a ride.

> When eight jobs and three careers become the norm for a working life, the spaces between the choices we make become as important as our performance on the job.

In the course of this trek, I've been fortunate enough to come across dozens of people who have done just that—men and women who are highly successful in their fields by any standard but who are special by virtue of their inner fluidity. I'll be introducing you to a number of them throughout these pages, sharing their stories so that you can find principles in them to guide your own journey. I'll also share the experience of working with several of the best of the new breed of "transition coaches," people trained to help us across the gaps that a life of almost constant innovation brings. Their services weren't cheap—my total bill would have come to $77,000 if I had paid full retail—but the experience was invaluable to me, and I hope to pass it on. Just as I'm convinced that in this rising world our most critical creation will be the design of our own lives, so I'm convinced that transition coaches are going to become as central to our professional and personal needs as trainers, executive coaches, and therapists are today.

A recent survey of executives reported that only one in five of us is in a job that we feel fits us well. I'm convinced we can do far better if we start viewing our entire professional life as a work in constant progress. Instead of seeing each position as an end in itself, we need to start thinking of the story of our work life as a succession of chapters. Just as each chapter of a book introduces different elements of the plot while still keeping to a central story line, so each chapter of our work lives can be devoted to a different aspect of who we are, what we aspire to, and how we want to live while still keeping to the central narrative of our own life. One chapter might be devoted to acquiring status and responsibility, another to acquiring wealth, another to teaching or serving our communities, another to focusing on our kids, another to learning something new, and yet another to making a major mark on the world with no expectation of personal gain.

> The story of our work lives is becoming a succession of chapters, each devoted to a different expression of our talents and aspirations.

We don't have to be all things at every moment to all people. It's in the totality that the book gets written, the story told. By seeking to live this way, by incorporating the principles of fluidity and reinvention into the very texture of our existences, I'm also convinced we can do a better job of finding satisfaction with our families along with a greater sense of personal freedom. I can speak with certainty only about myself, but both of those have been a central reason for me to embark on this search.

As the CEO of a public company, I came to see how these issues also have to be incorporated into the fabric of how we manage companies. The gold-watch model is dead and gone. We need to help the people who work for us come

to terms with a more tumultuous future. The best chief financial officer I have ever worked with was crippled not by a lack
of competence (he had tons of that) but by an inability to
enjoy the work because he couldn't access enough internal
fluidity to move with the uncertainties of a start-up business
in a start-up industry. We should have known more about how
to help him, but my experience across four industries and
companies large and small says that we weren't alone in lack-
ing the capacity to deal with such situations. The experience
motivated me to find better tools, and subsequently, we made
a number of limited experiments that allowed our people to
operate within this framework of chapters. Invariably, they
found themselves better able to navigate in an uncertain
world, even when that meant they navigated themselves right
out our door, to something much closer to the person they
were ready to become.

From all of these perspectives — the masters of change,
the transition coaches, my year of searching, my own wild six
years as a pioneer in the Internet revolution, what I now realize is my own lifetime of serial reinvention — I have found that
successfully embracing change seems to involve seven stages,
ranging from the recognition of the moment when change is
imminent, through a variety of steps by which we come to
master the change that first seems to be mastering us, to our
reemergence in a new zone of accomplishment and exhilaration, and finally to the cultivation of a capacity to leave well
so we can begin the entire process again. These seven stages
make up the core structure of this book (see the Stages of
Change on page 8). Collectively, they also form a natural
process that can be deployed time and again, and improved
upon each time we go through it.

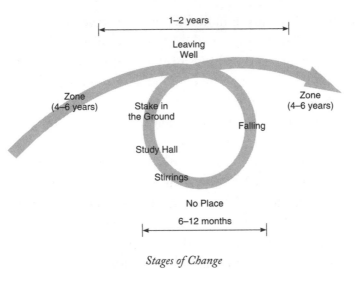

Stages of Change

These are not the proverbial seven steps to losing five pounds: These are powerful forces we are dealing with, accompanied by deep and often conflicting emotions. We don't give up where we have been easily; few of us can wander off into the wilderness without fearing what we might encounter and where we might land. Hard work is to be done at every stop along the way; the gaps in our lives demand as much attention as the periods of full engagement. But the process does work—in nature, in the arts, in psychology, even in new business development and corporate reinvention, and most importantly in our own lives.

> Learning to embrace and dance with change allows you to create a life of accomplishment and exhilaration.

Nobody was teaching these things 20 years ago when I was in business school. In 10 years, I'm convinced, the processes I'm writing about here will be part of the core curriculum of business education because the payoff will be so great: a succession of satisfying, rewarding, and customized opportunities by and through which to create an overall life you can be proud of, and the capacity to help others — your employees, your family, your friends — discover how to dance with change as well.

CHAPTER TWO

The Gig Is Up

*There is a time for departure, even when there's no
certain place to go.*

—Tennessee Williams

There's almost always a moment in old gangster movies
where you know the game is over. The feds have tightened
the noose. The place is surrounded. Ammo is running low
along with booze and cigars, and the thugs are thinning out,
too. Finally, Robinson or Cagney or whoever is on the lam
picks up the tommy gun, kisses the dame one last time, rises
up in front of the window, yells something like "Okay, you
dirty coppers, come and get me!" and begins blasting away
into the night. That's when the gig is up.

Truth told, the workplace isn't all that different. Whether
it's rum running or the numbers racket, applications for hand-
held wireless, advertising, automobiles, or teaching kids that
fills your days, there's no reward without risk, and risk means
winners and losers, upsides and downsides. There's no life
without dreaming, either. And dreaming means that people

will always bo looking at the workplace around them and thinking there's another place they would rather be, another job they would like to be doing, another life they would like to live. John Steinbeck said it far more poetically than I can in his saga of the Great Depression, *The Grapes of Wrath*: "Man, unlike any other thing organic or inorganic in the universe, grows beyond his work, walks up the stairs of his concepts, emerges ahead of his accomplishments."

What's different about all this isn't that the gig is up. Jobs, companies, aspirations, and dreams begin and end all the time. What's different is that the gig is up with a frequency that can seem almost constant, and that this time high rank and privilege are no protection against the onslaught of dislocation. The gig is up in this new world with a frighteningly democratic spirit. The average tenure of CEOs has fallen from 15 years to 9 years; the average professional job tenure, generally from 10 to 4 years, a drop of 60 percent in a single decade. The Center for Executive Options, which counsels and chronicles high-flying CEOs who have been fired or have terminated themselves, reports that the mean age of its clients has dropped from 56 to 46 years old. These are people who still have potentially three decades of professional life ahead, and three in five of them don't want to do anything related to the industries in which they once ran the show.

You're not alone if you feel you aren't in your dream job. Four out of five of us, at all job levels, say we aren't in the right job. About one in seven of us changes jobs every year.

Even in the most traditional callings, this tidal wave of change sweeps over the workplace. At the middle of the twentieth century, a minister at one of the mainline churches that make up the National Council of Churches could expect to spend a decade or more in the post, enough time to become an integral part of the community he served; enough time to baptize, confirm, and marry his parishioners, and bury some of their parents too; enough time even to call the parsonage home. Today, National Council of Churches ministers average about three years in each pulpit, burned out by a demanding vestry, or driven away by congregations that once deferred to the authority of the church and now claim it, or simply, like so many of the rest of us, struck by wanderlust, itchy feet, the desire to move on in the great American—and now global— smorgasbord.

Some of these changes are self-initiated. We move to follow a spouse or to follow some inner stirring which says it's time to go. We become wealthy, and this triggers a new set of motivations. Or like former Secretary of Labor Robert Reich, we burn out from 70-hour weeks on the job and too much time away from our family. Being Secretary of Labor in the Clinton White House can be every bit as tough as being Al Capone, especially when you have two boys at home wondering when and if they'll see you again.

Some changes, too, are thrust on us by events. Companies merge. Stock prices fall. School budgets get voted down. Political parties are voted out of office. Competitors come out of nowhere. In the compressed and accelerated cycles we all live in—product cycles, business cycles, company cycles, career cycles—people also just fall out of synch with what they do. Robert Levitan had already built his first company when he and I sat around my dining room table and put the finishing touches on the plan for iVillage. He cofounded the company with me and Nancy Evans, the former president and publisher of Doubleday, the publishing house. But Robert left us four years later on the eve of our initial public offering, not because we had bickered or he was angry but because what he did best was no longer what or where the company was. Robert was born for start-ups and the hard struggles of corporate infancy and early adolescence. In the old course of events, that process would have taken years. Under the new economic laws, we leapfrogged past that time in a relative instant, and as we did so, Robert came unstuck from us. Happily, he had the grace and wisdom to know it. More about "leaving well" later in the book.

Other changes, obviously, are imposed on us, whether we seek them or not. In a fiercely and globally competitive environment, office politics grow ever-more cutthroat and boards ever-more restive. A short horizon—for results, for profits, for market share—means a short fuse. A short shelf life—for companies as well as for the products they produce—means a high death rate. And it's always people, not the things they make or the services they perform, who get blown up in the final analysis.

> The ranks of successful CEOs are filled with men and women who have been unceremoniously dumped from previous jobs. The times we live in will not be known for job security, no matter how good you are.

But there's another great difference at work today, too. However the gig is up, it isn't always that bad. Ellen Hancock was fired from high-level positions at both Apple and IBM. Once upon a time, the second of those firings, if not the first, would have left Ellen toxic. Instead, she created Exodus and went on to become one of the world's wealthiest and most successful women entrepreneurs. Bob Pittman, one of the most gifted executives of our generation, was axed by Time Warner, the same company where he now serves as chief operating officer thanks to the marriage of his old company and America Online (AOL), where he had been brought in as president. The Matrix Awards are the highest honor given to women in the media; like the Oscars, they're voted by your peers. Four of the twelve women who received Matrix Awards at a recent ceremony mentioned being fired as one of the most important events to propel them forward in their careers. Michael Milken, the financier, took the idea of rising from the ashes to an extreme, passing through prison on his way to launching Knowledge Universe.

When the gig is up today, it's not up just a little bit. For most of us, it's up all the way. And that, I honestly believe, is the good news, not the bad, about the work world we all must live in. Change starts with endings, not beginnings. Something has to be over before something new can begin. The reinvention that I am convinced will be required of us all implies death as much as life. Whatever precipitates the change, what matters is what we do after these moments.

> There's the real model: It's how we use the momentum of disruption to propel us forward, how we use change to constantly align ourselves with who we are and who we are becoming, that makes all the difference.

"The gig is up," the gangsters said, and the credits rolled soon thereafter. "In my end is my beginning," T. S. Eliot wrote in the *Four Quartets*, and he still had two quartets to go.

Serial reinvention or serial disappointment? The choice belongs to each of us, all the time.

Outta Here

The first time I knew my own gig was up, I was 28 years old, living two-thirds of the year in a tent with my husband in some of the most beautiful mountains in the western United States, working for Outward Bound, and loving every moment of it. I carried my home on my back, baked bread over open fires, caught trout in the streams and cooked them for dinner, and slept under the stars every night. One day my husband and I were leading a group of professionals in a 90-day course that we had designed ourselves. I was sitting on a rock in the middle of a field on a crisp autumn day, and suddenly I knew I was done. I couldn't sit around another campfire. I'd seen the whole movie before. It would be a year and a half before I'd find myself in Boston, at Harvard Business School, but it was on that afternoon that the mountaineering chapter ended as surely as if I'd fallen off a cliff, and not just for me. My husband came to Boston with me—he took a graduate degree at Harvard's Kennedy School of Government while I was getting my MBA.

I had no glossary then for the way I was beginning to live; no concept of "chapters," of serial living; no sense of life as a book built by continual reinvention. I'd gone to the mountains maybe for much the same reason that Dustin Hoffman pursues Katharine Ross in *The Graduate*—out of love for the place I was headed to and because, caught between my father's insistence that I choose a career path and my own inability to commit to a lifetime's course at age 22, the mountains seemed like the only place that made sense. Only in the years since have I come to realize that for those of us who are lucky enough to know when to fire ourselves, there's almost always a moment, looking back, that tells us exactly what we are about to do.

Sometimes, the moment fills the present, unmistakable for anything else. Craig Cohon, whom you will meet later in this book, was a 37-year-old Coca-Cola executive, soon to be in charge of the European market, when he heard then President Clinton speak about the obligations of wealthy nations at the World Economic Forum, the annual assemblage of business, government, and religious leaders held at Davos, in the Swiss Alps. Before he fell asleep that night, Cohon knew that he would abandon his job to launch a new nonprofit group called Global Legacy. For him, the gig was up in the best of ways. As we'll see, his wife's gig was up at that moment, too. In the complicated ballet of life and work, that's beautiful symmetry.

More often, the moments that herald the end of a chapter are in a code that can be more obvious to others than it is to us. Donald Marrs—author of *Executive in Passage*, a riveting, sometimes emotionally brutal account of his own experiments in serial living—tells of growing a beard several months after receiving a prestigious promotion to senior management at the Chicago headquarters of his ad firm, Leo Burnett. Marrs had asked for a downward transfer to the agency's Los Angeles production group so that he could begin his dream of breaking into film before he saw the beard for what it was: a visual breakpoint for the deeper break he was preparing to make. His beard said the gig was up before he was able to interpret the inaudible sounds.

One friend, a senior editor at a national magazine, tells of being required to box up all his books and other artifacts in preparation for an office-wide rehab. He was getting ready to reshelve the books when he noticed that he had labeled some boxes "A" and others "B." The "A" books, he realized, were ones he intended to take with him when he left; the "B" boxes were filled with books he was willing to leave behind. A month later, he was self-employed, starting to write the books he had always intended to write.

Linda Blank, who was forced into a life of serial reinvention by circumstances and learned to use it to shape a successful future for herself, was in her early twenties, living in Israel with her sister, when her life collapsed on her as she was looking for a new apartment.

"I was killing myself physically with the schedule that I had to do," Linda told me. "I was trying to learn the language, trying to hold down this job. I was living in a new immigrants' dormitory where no one else was working. Then one day my sister and I went to look at an apartment in Tel Aviv. We were walking through it, and my sister was saying, 'Well, this is a possibility.' Afterwards I walked outside and said to her, 'Why do I have to live this way? If we took an apartment like this in New York, we'd be out of our goddamned minds and we'd know it. I'm leaving. I'm going home.'"

A month later, Linda was on a plane, heading back to America with no money and no job waiting. As so often happens with the critical changes in our lives, what had been tolerable moments before—the work, the living conditions, the distance from home—was intolerable the moment the end of the gig announced itself.

I knew intellectually that I was ready to leave the corporate world of Time Warner, even though I was president of Time-Life Video and Television, with lots of creative latitude and an Emmy under my belt. I sensed that I wanted to head into a more self-expressive, entrepreneurial world, but I knew it for certain only after I opened my suitcase at the resort where Time Inc.'s annual executive retreat was being held and saw what I had packed. Khaki shorts and polo shirts were de rigueur for the field games that were meant to be a bonding experience at these affairs. But there was no uniform of the day in my suitcase—only a flashy t-shirt and a pair of black spandex shorts that, truth told, looked great on me. Similarly, there was an expected look for the big party that capped the event on the last night: for men, a suit of obvious expense but muted style; for women, much the same, in black. As I hung up the magenta Versace I'd brought along for the affair, I said to myself, well, this is it. I'm outta here. A few days later I bought an Hermes jacket that practically broke my bank. I knew even as I handed the salesperson my plastic that it was a jacket I would never wear into Time Warner headquarters, and a week after that I was gone.

Sometimes, too, the moments that tell us the gig is up just plain blindside us, like sucker punches when we're looking somewhere else. A career and a half after Time Warner, in the fall of 1999, Nancy Evans and I were in our fifth year of building the most successful women's online network in the world—purely in that magical Zone of creation, where everything comes together so completely you can forget time and place—when Nancy suddenly felt her own gig was up. In an effort to keep her committed for another year or two, until the company was safely out of the woods, I asked Jim Taylor, a consultant and good friend, to come up to New York from his home in Santa Fe.

Nancy had been fantasizing about escaping Manhattan, where she has lived for 15 years, for a slower country life, someplace with acres of grass that she could sit on a lawn tractor and mow to her heart's content. To let her try out the idea and to get away from the phones and all the day-to-day pressures of running a start-up, the three of us rented a car, headed off to leafy Greenwich, Connecticut, and absolutely made the day of the real estate agent we popped in on. A choice property in Greenwich? But of course, Madam!

I saw it all as a kind of therapy for Nancy, a way that she could get back to work but have her eye on the light at the end of the tunnel. Maybe it even worked: Nancy is still with iVillage as I write, still vital to its success. But the true therapeutic value, I found, was not for Nancy but for me. It was my gig that was up, not hers. Almost literally out of the blue as I stood on those country lawns, I could begin to feel the glue coming off my life. For five years I'd been attracted to the kind of moguls I had now become, but suddenly they had no power over me, no lure or magnetism. Since 1995, almost literally everything I had done had been in the interest of building iVillage. Now, in a matter of weeks, doing so really annoyed me. Things that hadn't tired me for half a decade exhausted me. Things that had never frustrated me in the Zone now frustrated me to the point of screaming, or tears.

I couldn't leave the company immediately—there was a new CEO to find, a process of succession to plan—but I was ready in that instant to let it all go, and ready also to enrich a personal life that I'd left hanging on the hook too much of the time. I wasn't willing to pay the price anymore of relationships with men who could never escape the fact that I was a CEO. My assistant was spending more time on the phone with my boyfriend than I was; she was even transcribing his love notes. And I was especially ready to be there for my children now that they had begun to complain about my absences and articulate their own rights to my time. Michaela was turning six, and Ellie was already five. Getting to their recitals had been enough before. Now I was desperately missing everything—buying them saddle shoes, picking out Halloween costumes—because the ground under me had shifted as it eventually shifts for almost all of us.

> Learn to read the small signs. A new haircut, an unexpectedly strong reaction to a book or movie, even a canceled subscription might be telling you that you are about to call in well.

Here Today, Gone Tomorrow

It's not just employees who come unglued from their callings. Sometimes businesses and the people who launch and staff them come unglued, too, caught like everything else in cycles that are compressed almost beyond recognition, in an economy that never seems to rest.

Katherine Legatos is almost an entire history of the dot-com industry. Trained at Estée Lauder and Jim McCann's 1-800-Flowers, Katherine was one of the first 10 people Nancy Evans and I hired at iVillage, in 1995. Four years later, in the spring of 1999, she left us to form her own company—ingredients.com. The idea was very much of the time: to create a niche online retail site, in this case an e-store selling high-end beauty and personal-care products, and to marry it with advertising in one of those synergistic unions that were at the heart of the dot-com dream. For a while it even looked as if Katherine might make it. Then came the April 2000 industry meltdown, and instead of being the entrepreneur who was building her vision, Katherine became the other person that an entrepreneur must also be: the one who keeps the vision alive to the very end, when there's nothing left but fumes to run on.

In the course of a scant 19 months, until she closed ingredients.com for good on September 26, 2000, Katherine had lived an entire corporate cycle—creating a business plan, raising money, building a product line, manufacturing it, getting it to customers (and she did), building customer loyalty (and she did that, too), and then nearly at the peak of her success beginning to dismantle everything she had created, knowing the end must come but never allowing herself to admit it until there was nothing left at all, and the gig was up with an unmistakable finality. Her story is instructive.

"It was the fastest ride up," Katherine told me when we got together a few months after her business had gone under. "In fact, it happened in such a short time that I still can't believe it. There were a wonderful eight or nine months of creative development work that I'll treasure forever. I worked with wonderful people in creating ingredients. Then as soon as we founded it and started this incredibly fast-paced process of assembling staff and systems, things began to fall apart.

"By January 2000 we had to make the first decision to lay off—15 out of 50 people. Then in April came the second decision, another 25 people. January through September 26, when I closed the operations, became this very slow process, this fight for survival. On the last day, I was still thinking that there was a chance. I think that was necessary—I had to do that. The last morning before we closed it, I told all the employees there was a 50-50 chance we'd survive. I knew that it wasn't 50-50, but I was going to consider it 50-50 because I had to for the sake of the company, of the people who were left.

"I'd gone to sleep the night before saying, 'On Tuesday morning, we've just got to find a way to get another $50,000.' When we couldn't make that payment on Tuesday at noon, that was it. Our shipping threatened to shut us down. We couldn't let our customers be charged for the product and then not be able to get the product to them. We just had to quit."

Katherine Legatos didn't make it, but she had plenty of company in the dot-com world as once blindly optimistic investors began to race for the door. By September, when Katherine pulled the plug on ingredients, another 100-plus dot-com companies had experienced major layoffs, and many of those were facing the same downward curve of dwindling hope that she had faced. Over 200 Internet companies shut down in 2000. Business cycles once resembled sine curves: There was almost a stateliness to them. Now, they looked more like the polygraph test of a compulsive liar, and at the end of each sharp downward slash, the gig was up across the board.

Bang, Bang, You're Fired

My dad is probably a lot like a lot of your fathers and grand-fathers. He grew up, went to college, got a job, and spent his whole career with one company and his whole life with one woman, my mom, until her death. Dad had one set of kids and pretty much one set of ideas. He retired at age 65 and may have died of golf 10 years later. A warm and sparkling Irishman, dad didn't write his own life. Like your parents and grandparents, his life was written for him in the unspoken expectations of his generation.

Sure, the quality of relationships varied. There were the linear scorecards of money, title, and property to help determine who won and lost. Despite the stereotype, these weren't cookie-cutter lives. What's more, these were good people — people who had fought a world war and won it, people who had grown up in the shadow of the Great Depression and come out the other side of both deprivation and conflict with hope and dignity still intact. My siblings and I were well cared for, lucky in many ways. But basically, my father and his generation of white-collar workers were asked to do their best on the conveyor belt of human existence, and that's what they did. Like the industrial economy they served, they were mass-produced, and because they were, they lived inside a world of sureties, a place of confident assertions. Of them, none was more certain than this: that there was no worse fate than termination. One day you were working your way up the corporate ladder, accruing salary, angling for better office space; the next day, you existed forever after in a state of eternal and unshakable shame.

Today, those same rules and conditions simply don't apply. Yes, of course, getting fired still can be a blow to the ego. Yes, it can still have a devastating effect on the personal bottom line, although not as devastating on average as one might first think. U.S. Department of Labor statistics suggest that among white-collar workers who were downsized out of their jobs in recent years and subsequently rehired, more than a quarter saw their wages grow by more than 20 percent; another quarter earned up to 20 percent more than they had been making. But getting fired can also be an opportunity, a chance to escape a past we have grown tired of or unproductive in, a goad to try new roads that we may only dimly realize are waiting for us. Used creatively, termination can be the new beginning so many of us privately long for.

Half of all those who are fired make the same or more money afterward. Some make exponentially more, faster, and with much less effort. Let's make sure you are among them.

Bill Strickland, a master of the serial life about whom much more will be said later, had a vision of himself—an epiphany, call it what you will—as a commercial pilot. He had no background in any of the air military services, as most commercial pilots do. He had no particular preparation for the vocation at all. In fact, he'd been trained as an artist. Nor did he have any excess salary to indulge his whims. At the time he launched his flying career, Strickland was earning a very mid-five-figure salary managing a craft center in the Manchester section of Pittsburgh, a once-elegant inner-city neighborhood that had succumbed to hard times decades earlier. But Strickland simply knew that he had to fly jumbo jets—it had come to him with the power of revelation—and to accumulate the training, hours, and other credentials so he could get there, he bought a plane when his contemporaries were just finding their way into the starter homes of the real estate market.

"I said I'm going to fly these planes, period. It's not about 'maybe.' It's about 'when.' I'm going to fly a jet before I leave this planet, and somebody is going to hire me to do it. It was a question of getting the experience and being trained, so I took basically the majority of my salary. I bought a plane, and the plane, really, it's like a mortgage payment. Instead of buying a house, I bought an airplane. I paid monthly, and the plane was available so I could build flight time. I went off to 727 school on my own."

And it worked. Strickland accumulated the necessary hours. He passed the requisite tests. In time, he even found just what he had dreamed for himself: a job as a commercial pilot with a global carrier. The problem was that Braniff, the airline he landed a job with, was unable to compete in the newly deregulated air-passenger industry. Ten years after Strickland first took the controls of a Braniff passenger jet, the airline laid him off and then closed its doors for good, and Bill Strickland was out on the street, too old by then to be hired on as a pilot anywhere new. It should be a tragic tale; as we'll see, it's not. Bill would go on, after a rough period of self-discovery, to launch one of the great social ventures of our times, one he is now replicating across the country. But the Braniff story points to a larger truth. Most firings aren't personal in this new world unless we take them personally. Most firings are just the price of business in a business world cut free of artificial constraints.

The acceleration of mergers, of business cycles, and of global competition has made the numbers almost legendary. Gold standards of the computer products industry find their markets shrinking, and suddenly tens of thousands of workers, all across the spectrum, are out on the street. Telecommunications giants merge, and almost 100,000 workers go out on strike, afraid for their jobs, their pay, and their retirement security. Old and honored names—Montgomery Ward, Oldsmobile, Pan Am—simply cease to exist. IBM, the epitome for decades of corporate paternalism, launched the current deluge in 1992–1993 when it responded to shrinking profits and market share by chopping 120,000 "lifetime employees" from its payrolls. Add dependents and spouses to those 120,000 people and you'd have a good-size city. And it's not just the corporate world where dislocation reigns. HMOs have turned healthcare delivery upside down and sent thousands of doctors and nurses fleeing from a profession they once loved. Family farms have disappeared by the tens of thousands in the last 15 years, overthrowing a way of life that is generations old.

Some of us die from exposure, unprotected by normal custom and usage as we once were, or unable to protect ourselves in the newly Darwinian work world. Others die by small degrees, unable to find a fit into businesses, whole industries, and work environments that seem to change our terms and conditions by the hour. Either way the bodies mount and mount and mount, and as they do, the sheer numbers offer a kind of refuge that we have to learn to take advantage of. Getting fired, riffed, downsized, laid off, whatever we call it, isn't what it used to be. It's no longer about the conversation around us. It's about the conversation in our own heads, what we say to ourselves, and that is far easier to change—and very much part of what this book is about.

It's okay to be between jobs. Instead of avoiding these gaps, relish and deploy them.

Firing Yourself

The terminated have no choice: They're out on the street. But what is it that encourages those of us who do have options to leave a job or a work life that we've outlived or to stay when all the silent signs are telling us to go? Burnout is certainly a factor. Just as happened with me at iVillage, many of us don't know how tired we truly are until we first admit that we might be tired at all. In the Zone, tiredness simply isn't an option; out of it, it can be everything.

Practical matters play a role, too. When Congress created the 401(k) plan, it helped make pension benefits portable. For companies, 401(k)s and their cousins were a way out of onerous lifetime associations, but portable benefits are also not to be ignored when employees are struck with wanderlust. I have no idea whether my dad had a secret dream of himself as a welder or stage designer or schoolteacher — most men in those days kept that conversation to themselves — but even if he had, dad was tied to his employer by more than custom and usage. The funding for his golden years depended on his allegiance to the company and on the company's continued beneficence to those who were faithful to its cause. Today, we can roll our benefits over into another 401(k), a Keogh, an IRA, or a variety of other options. Perhaps without even realizing it was doing so, Congress gave us wings if we choose to take flight.

The robust economy of the last decade of the twentieth century didn't hurt either. The 1990s made many of us rich not only in purely monetary ways but in choice as well and in a propensity to accept risk; and choice and wealth and bent of mind all matter. It's easier listening to that inner voice when there's a soft place to land. The inner voices also speak to us more clearly when we're predisposed to hear them.

I used to think of this simply as a fear of change, but David Zelman, one of my transition coaches and someone who has helped hundreds of highly successful people initiate transitions, says that in his work he has found that people don't fear or even mind change. They welcome it, in fact. What they dread and hate above all else is the void that accepting change threatens to plunge them into. It's that uncertainty—not knowing what lies ahead, not having faith that the next thing will be better than or even as good as the last thing—that keeps them hanging on to the old, even when they know in their hearts that they are on the backside of enjoyment and creativity.

Just as we still lack a complete language to discuss the mega-change that is upon us, so we also lack the rituals to help us through it. Bill Bridges, the author of *Transitions*, one of the wisest books on this subject, talks about the ironic differences between our current culture—inundated with transitions yet terrified of their discomforts—and more traditional cultures, where change was both much more rare and much more subject to well-established rituals that acknowledged the discomfort and eased members through the breakpoints.

That doesn't mean that every retirement party has to be accompanied by a male drumming chorus in full animal skins or that every promotion deserves to be lauded by human sacrifice. But by ignoring the significance of such moments, by failing to treat them externally in a way consistent with the internal processes that accompany them, we create a work world top heavy with weird disconnects and oddly uncomfortable functions. One friend tells of ending her 24-year association with a publication—an association that had produced numerous major prizes—with a cake and ice cream party squeezed into an afternoon deadline schedule.

"At the end, I helped one of the interns take the leftover ice cream back to the refrigerator and got some hot water and paper towels to help clean up. I couldn't leave that mess behind. Then I popped my nameplate off the front of my office, walked over to the St. Regis, and spent $29 for two glasses of cabernet in the lobby. I was sitting there, all by myself, well into the second glass, when it suddenly dawned on me that I might not ever walk into that office again. Twenty-four years, and that was it. Who would I ever have lunch with again?"

Mastering the Game

Whether we're jumping from rock to rock across a streambed, stepping from beam to beam in an unfinished skyscraper, or leaping across an ice crevasse 27,000 feet up on a Himalayan glacier, a fundamental principle of physical law and human nature obtains: It's not the takeoff or the landing spots that scare us, but the space between them. As David Zelman's work suggests—and as everyone's gut-checks will confirm—the same is true of change in work and life. We are geared in our society for forward motion, for upward mobility, for action and achievement. Yet if we can expect to have eight or more serious jobs and three careers in an average adult working life and if that working life is going to get longer and longer (about 13 percent of Americans over the age of 65 now work, a figure that has been rising steadily), we will be doing a lot of leaping from a lot of hard ground over a mighty number of gaps, some no wider than the space between train and platform and some more in the nature of a yawning abyss.

One of the premises of this book is that to succeed in this process, it is the gaps we must begin to concentrate on. We're already good at giving ourselves fully to what we do. Where the muscles need development is in the times between when we're gathering our energies and pointing our resources toward what comes next. That's when the real work comes; that's when we have to listen to what the inner voices are saying. We can never truly master change until we learn to breathe to the rhythms of the spaces between our landings, accepting the fear and sometimes raw terror those spaces bring, and moving on and through them.

This book, in short, offers no shortcuts, no panaceas, no magic pills. If you're looking for those, head back to the bookstore. I don't think there are any shortcuts. Just as traditional transition rites are hard work—nights and days alone in the desert, a week of celebration, another week of grief, physical mutilation, and the like—so the spaces between the changes of our lives are hard work, too. We've all known people who have rushed too quickly back into a new job after getting fired from an old one, and we've known people who have waited too long. Everyone's experience is different, but in my own experience, the people who rush through the gap—who leap to the next gig as soon as the last one is up—are the ones who ultimately suffer the most because they miss out on a future that could be made just for them alone.

Money

We all need to eat. We humans like a roof over our heads. Inevitably, money matters when a gig ends, however the end arrives. We'll be returning to this subject over and over throughout the book because it evolves with the entire process of reinvention. For now, keep in mind this advice: We don't have to give our heart until we want to. If you need to go back to work immediately, try to think of it as a lease, not a sale. I've done it via consulting. Teacher friends have done it by substituting; journalist friends by freelancing. When we were slaving away for Barry Diller at Q2, we used to dream of jobs at Tastee-Freez. One of his famous protogés did in fact do a McDonald's gig after being fired by Rupert Murdoch. One childhood friend fleeing a desk job worked for four months as a landscaper. He got sun and exercise. Far more important, he got the time to begin inventing a new life for himself—the greatest of luxuries at these turning points. What's more, as you get more accustomed to the rhythms of change in your life, it becomes far easier to plan for what lies ahead, and that includes financial planning.

What seemed to be a tidbit of money advice my dad gave me turned out to be profound. Keep a year's worth of living expenses liquid, he told me: It'll help; you never know what will happen. After a divorce disrupted my plans for funding Harvard Business School and I had run through all the scholarship money available, I asked a sweet little lady sitting behind the desk in the financial aid office what I could do. Use your credit card, she advised, and that's when I knew how right my dad had been.

At first, building up a reserve fund wasn't easy. I came out of business school with a debt load twice the size of my first salary. But I scrimped here and saved there. Every time I got a tax refund, in it went to the rainy-day account before I could get to the stores to reward myself. Every bonus went there, too, and every tiny windfall from aunts and uncles. Eventually, I had six months of living expenses saved up; in time, six months became the year my dad always wanted me to have.

What I was buying with my cash reserve was peace of mind, in part. Far more important, though, and without my ever knowing it in the early days, I was buying the time to see the gaps in my life through to their end, and the more time I bought for those gaps, the richer the reward has been. Still, in a quarter century of working, I never took a break longer than three months. This time, I've taken nine months, drawing down that rainy-day fund I built, refusing even handsome offers to get back into the battle—and the results qualitatively have been completely different.

Airline pilots will say that if you're three degrees off in your heading between, say, New York and Hartford, it won't make a huge difference. You'll still get to central Connecticut; once you're there, Hartford isn't hard to find. But if you're three degrees off in your heading between New York and Los Angeles, you can end up over San Francisco or well into Mexico. That's what this cash reserve is all about: You're buying as much time as you can to make sure you have the heading right, to make sure

In a world this uncertain, a year's salary in the bank is worth anything you have to give up to get there.

you're on the way to where you want to go. That takes time. Time takes money. And the more life becomes an alternation between being ultimately involved in the work we are doing and using the spaces between work to reposition our compasses, the more valuable that money becomes.

Fire or Ice

One more thing to keep in mind about mastering this game: We get to the end of our gigs by different routes, some more painful than others, some indeed almost unbearable, but when we're airborne between now and what's to come, however wide the chasm we're crossing, we're all subject to the same downward pull of gravity. Big bodies and small bodies, wide ones and narrow ones, happy ones and sad ones—we all fall at exactly 32 feet per second squared.

Bill Bridges tells the story of a man given a major promotion who then had to report to a whole new set of superiors. The new responsibilities meant more hours, and the longer hours inevitably hurt his relationship with his children. There was more money, too, and the spouse he had less time to attend to used it to finance a major remodeling of their home. (Consumption in these cases is often communication, my friend Jim Taylor contends.) Family camping was out the window; golf weekends with his new business associates were in. Substitute for a major promotion a major firing, a major separation, a major anything, and while the details might change, the emotional effect is not likely to be much different.

The point I'm hoping to make here is that whatever process sets off the end of a chapter, the variations of the gig is up are far more similar than different. Magnitude matters, but often less than you might think. Self-esteem counts, but we all come down to the same questions. Whether we step up or step down or just step across to another equal place, we've still got the space in between to deal with, and it's only by changing the conversation in our heads about that space, by understanding its shape and its duration, that we can create the road map that will tell us where we are and where we are going.

We need new transition rituals, not ones made for primitive societies. We need rituals that will increase our comfort level with the world of change we live in, ones that will help us deal with getting fired, deal with corporate flameout, deal with firing ourselves, deal with letting go of a beloved job to support a spouse's move. We need a guidebook that will help us navigate a new century in which constant transition promises to be the norm, one that will help us use this inevitable change to pilot our own way to success and freedom, not as they are defined by others but as they are defined deep within each of us. Just as important, we need a guidebook to help us better understand what our families, friends, and colleagues are going through when they are in these precious and often initially painful gaps in their lives, and help them understand us when we're the ones in the middle.

I intend for this to be that guide, and not just for individuals. Anyone who runs a company or a large organization needs to understand this as well. All of our institutions must create the internal fluidity that will allow for the rapid deployment and redeployment of workers, because if they don't, their best talent is going to rapidly and fluidly deploy and redeploy themselves right out of town. There's a force out there, a force building and growing. Unless institutions learn to master it, unless they learn to make their organizations breathe to its rhythms just as each of us must learn to breathe to its rhythms, they'll end up staffed largely by people who are afraid to make the leaps required of modern life.

It's worth repeating: When the gig is up, it's up all the way. And that really, really, really is all right. There's hell ahead: We'll get to that in a minute. Self-doubt, walks in the desert, homework: Only some of it is fun, and even that means passing through pain. We're setting off on a journey here. We're going to go step by step together through some difficult and hard times—believe me, I've field-tested this process—but at the end lies the promise of reinvention. At the end lies a life that doesn't try to be all things at once but offers instead the chance to do everything we want to do as well as we can do it. At the end, I think, lies a whole new way of looking at ambition, service, mentoring, retirement, planning, even marriage and child rearing—the things that matter, in the ways that matter. Now, let's deal with the worst of it right at the get-go.

CHAPTER THREE

Falling

*One must be thrust out of a finished cycle in life,
and that leap is the most difficult to make—to
part with one's faith, when one would rather
renew the faith and recreate the passion.*

—Anais Nin

Carole Hyatt sold her research business after her partner died suddenly of a heart attack, and then she went home and essentially didn't get dressed for six months. When people asked her what she did, she would stumble around before finally saying she was a "lunchist." The brother of a good friend pocketed nearly $10 million when the manufacturing firm he had stuck with through thick and thin was picked off by its chief competitor. Rich beyond his wildest imaginings, he went to his beach cottage and stopped answering the phone for a month. It was the only place, he told me later, where he felt as if there was something solid under his feet.

No one I know fell further or faster than Eric. He'd been a professional artist for 15 years, struggling all the way. To support himself, Eric had driven cabs and worked as an icer in a bakery. Finally, at age 39, he was just starting to break through, getting into shows not only in the East, where he lived, but all across the country. To celebrate this first real taste of success, Eric and his girlfriend had joined a Caribbean cruise. They were just off the coast of Panama when Eric broke his pelvis and both arms in a water-skiing accident.

For Eric, the sense of suspended animation that permeates this falling process was literal. For two weeks, he was held in total traction in Panama. For another six months, he was virtually immobilized in a Los Angeles hospital, not well enough to travel home, not mobile enough even to brush his own teeth. Eric's artwork was physical as well as imaginative. It involved large, interactive pieces. Now, it seemed possible he would never walk again. As far as he was concerned, he says, the career that he had struggled so hard to establish was over.

"I can remember lying there and asking myself, 'What are you now? Who are you?' I really had no idea," he told me.

Ironically, he says, it was a call from an art dealer whom he never got along with that turned everything around. "No one was contacting me at the hospital. I seemed to have stopped existing as far as the art world was concerned. Then this dealer called and said—and I remember her exact words—'You'll remember this time when your phone is ringing off the hook again.'"

When Eric and I talked the other day, he was heading off to Venice, to oversee the installation of one of his pieces in the Biennale di Venezia, one of the art world's global showcases. Falling stories do have happy endings—they're just so hard to imagine at the moment.

Katherine Legatos remembers the end of ingredients.com in vivid terms:

"A month after the operation shut down, I'd meet with people, and they would start apologizing. It was really very nice. They'd sit across the table from me and apologize and apologize, and I'd say, 'You know, it's okay. It's tough, but it's okay.'

"I felt awkward having to deal with it, but these people were very close to me, and they had watched me work so hard. I'd put everything into it, and it had been taken away from me. It's like someone's dying. I wonder if all this has to do with losing a sense of identity. You have so much of your identity that's tied to the company.

"Calling people who had invested their money in the company was really tough. With the first few of them, I couldn't keep a straight voice. Afterwards, I'd go to bed and not want to get up. For at least a week solid, I wasn't good for anything. Then a weird thing happened. I started to feel a sense of relief. All of a sudden, I was not responsible for anybody. People weren't watching me and wondering if I was going to save them or not. I didn't have to go to work every day and get on the phone and wait for someone to reject us. All of the things that I was responsible for were gone. Now, I could sit for a full day, or go watch a movie, or do nothing. I might not even get dressed.

"I felt guilty, totally felt guilty. In fact, I remember picking up the phone with this somewhat happy voice, and if the call was from an investor, I would immediately feel this terrible sense of guilt, like 'What was I doing, being okay?' And that was interspersed with these feelings that I couldn't control. Sometimes I was okay, sometimes I wasn't. I was really embarrassed, too. I mean, I had failed, and I had to face it.

"Your friends and your colleagues look at you in a certain way. Then you start to get fewer phone calls. You know, things don't happen as much. People don't want to go out with you all of a sudden. I don't think they mean it, but after that first line of phone calls to say, 'I'm sorry,' your phone's not ringing like it used to be. That's when you start to feel like, 'Oh, my God. My company. I failed. I'll never be able to do it again. I'm worthless. Who's going to want me?' But even then, there is this kind of sense of self that keeps you going."

Falling is less about actual falling than this sensation of falling. Imagine for a moment that you were able to freeze-frame yourself in the act of leaping the gap between the chapter you have been living and the often unknown place you are headed to next. And then imagine that you were able to step out of the freeze-frame and look down. Everything you would experience in that moment is what you are likely to experience now: disorientation; a sense of weightlessness; like Katherine Legatos, a kind of manic alternation between elation for escaping the old life, self-doubt about shaping a future, and often a sense of failure crushing enough to fill the seemingly bottomless pit you are crossing. All of it seems personal, and much of it truly is, even the money. Better than 20 percent of all venture capital comes from individuals and families, not faceless financial institutions.

Face it: You're lost in space. Whether you sold your company, liberated yourself, or got shown the door, the disorientation is the same. Am I Mr. Big? Or Mr. Nobody?

Inescapably, there's raw fear to deal with, too, no matter what has brought you to this moment. You're not who you were; you're not yet who you are becoming. I've found there's also a kind of welcomed numbing, particularly in the early days and weeks, that allows you to tell yourself and your friends that everything is going to be just fine. And the truth is that whether it is a self-eviction to follow a dream, a corporate failure, or just some politics you could no longer bear that has launched you, there will be many such freeze-frame events in the days and weeks, maybe even months, ahead; many such moments when guilt, overwhelming relief, and a simply welcome dullness of sensation will all seem to tumble over and around each other like clothes in a dryer.

My friend Karen Quinn, who survived for 15 years in the competitive waters of American Express and did so with great grace, was let go suddenly and for no reason in a cyclical workforce reduction. When I called her the next day, she said that she felt pretty good about it all. Deep down, she had known for some time that this was the right thing for her but couldn't motivate herself to leave on her own. For her, she told me philosophically, this was the only way she could have left. Two days later, when I called again, she was devastated; a few days after that, totally excited about all the time with her children; another few days down the road, panic-stricken about all the time with her children. And so it went. A friend calling every Friday would have thought this whole business was a snap for her. A friend calling only on Tuesdays might well have called the suicide hotline on her behalf.

Donald Marrs reports much the same clanging of seemingly antithetical emotions when he finally pulled the plug on his life as a Leo Burnett ad executive shortly after winning a big promotion and began the leap toward his next life as a filmmaker. Not long after he left the agency, Marrs writes, he found himself wandering among the coastal haunts of southern California:

"As I walked along the crowds of Venice Beach, I saw the downsides of what I was trying to do. . . . Had some of these people been hard-working executives at some time? Was I closer to fulfillment now than when I was working on the Jolly Green Giant account, or was I simply another loser? Or was I just being born? . . . Deep down, I felt I was being born, but I also felt I was dying. I just didn't know which would happen first."

One more point to be made here: You may be leaving a position where you set the schedule or were required to live by one, even a position where others were required to live by the whims of your own clock. But believe me, all this is going to happen on its own timetable.

In 1989, I went to help Barry Diller build a new kind of media company that would bring home shopping to normal people. I didn't go to work for Q2 out of any great zeal for cubic zirconium—I got enough of that at my going-away party at Time-Life—or, for that matter, any enormous love for Q2's parent organization, QVC. I went because I was getting ready for the entrepreneurial chapter of my life that would find its realization with iVillage, and Q2 was being run by one of the greatest and most demanding media entrepreneurs to be found anywhere in the world at that time: Barry Diller. And for a while the whole thing almost worked, although I never admitted to my friends that I was running a home shopping channel.

The team we assembled at Q2—pros from Saks Fifth Avenue, CNN, Conde Nast, the Gap, and elsewhere—got behind our project with almost messianic zeal. Within six months we went from literally nothing to a studio producing live television 24 hours a day, 7 days a week, with a huge retail operation behind it, all overseen from a century-old bakery called Silver Cup across the river from Manhattan. We were all in the Zone, going 100 miles an hour . . . into what proved an absolute brick wall. Following a lifelong dream, Barry bought CBS. Moments after the deal was announced, Barry was in his office celebrating, surrounded by orchids and letters of congratulations and armed with plenty of wine, when Comcast stepped in, blocked the sale, and bought Barry out instead. And that was all the opening QVC, which never could stand "the Diller kids," needed. While I was off in Las Vegas giving a speech, QVC fired every one of my people—talented pros—and sent guards to walk them out the door, that perverted ritual by which we mark final moments in our litigious culture. I walked out the door not many days later.

I knew I should be feeling grief about all this, but for four weeks I felt nothing but relief. Where was the funeral all my friends seemed to think I should be attending? Q2 was over, done with—and thank God, I could move on, and was I ever ready to! A month afterward, I was in Aspen, skiing and looking after my then baby daughter, when my own foundation fell out as completely as if the earth had opened up beneath me. Intellectually, I knew that getting fired in such a situation was almost a badge of honor. Intellectually, I knew also that I was ready to take the next step: I'd learned enough, and I already had the raw outlines for iVillage on paper and in my bones. But the intellect and the heart don't always travel in tandem. Like Katherine Legatos and Donald Marrs, I felt worthless.

Just as bad, I was overwhelmed with sadness for the accomplished people I'd brought to Q2, the pros who had been sent packing. And I felt something else also that most of us are reluctant to talk about but that was just as real and powerful as any of the other emotions that roiled through me in those dark days: an anger, at times murderous in its intensity, and maybe all the worse because it had been so long building before it got to the surface.

Tough it out. "Falling" ranks with kidney stones on the global fun chart, but if you can get through this without bailing, the rest is fun.

It would be nice, of course, if you could set your watch to these gap crossings. In reality, this schedule is a lot more like trying to fly out of New York's LaGuardia airport: maybe on time, maybe not, maybe today, maybe tomorrow, depending on the weather and the air traffic overhead. However we get there, though, whenever we get there, from whatever circumstance set us on this journey, we'll all arrive at pretty much the same place eventually.

Where Am I?

In his pioneering work on transitions, Bill Bridges provides a highly useful taxonomy of the different passages you can expect to go through in this falling phase. First is the process of disengagement, the feeling that you've been ripped out of your familiar place in the social order. Ancient cultures often formalized this procedure with the trek: 40 days in the desert, solo journeys by sea, climbing to the mountaintop. Whatever the underlying myths and sets of beliefs, the fundamental purpose held constant: To get to where he was going, the hero had to fall into nowhere, to come unmoored from who and what he had been. In the "no-place," he could begin building a new place and person again. So it still is today.

One friend tells of attending summer camp when he was 13 years old. It was his fourth summer there, the last one he would spend at the camp, and in the final week, he was tapped for a secret honor society just as the bugle blew lights out. Blindfolded, he was led through the woods to a small clearing, where the blindfold was removed and a masked counselor handed him a pack of matches and a blanket. He was to build a fire and keep it going all night, the counselor told him. If he failed, if he fell asleep, he wouldn't be inducted. When the same counselor returned in the morning, this time without his mask, my friend was sitting by a roaring blaze, wrapped in the blanket against the dawn chill.

"It's strange. I don't have any memory of how I stayed awake or what I thought about—I was scared to death mostly—but I remember that night like it was yesterday. I'd just hit puberty; I didn't know what the hell was going on with me. But I went into that woods at the end of my boyhood, and I came out at the beginning of manhood. And I think I knew, too, that even though I'd spent some of the happiest months of my life at that camp, I was never going to come back."

Maybe the hardest thing of all in this disengagement period is to simply honor the process in yourself and in your friends. After finding that her own business "success" felt like failure, Carole Hyatt wrote *When Smart People Fail* with coauthor Linda Gottlieb to explore the process by which people experience and move past setbacks. In the book, Carole reminds us that these early moments out of the gate are no time for dispensing great advice. If it's a friend who has jettisoned an old life, think of him less as someone looking for a place to land than as a person in a kind of waking shock — in need maybe of a beer, a hug, an extra ticket to the movies or a ball game, a walk along the canal, but not the unified theory of how he should lead the rest of his life. He doesn't know what the rest of his life will or should or can be at this point.

The magnitude of the letting go, the sonic boom that accompanied the departure, isn't the issue here, either. Believe it or not, someone who has just sold his business for $100 million is likely to be undergoing the same sense of disengagement and loss as someone who was just fired. The external reference points of life have disappeared; there are no new ones yet to take their place. Money, success, fame is no protection against that: A king can be just as lost in a maze as a pauper. My months with a paper net worth of nine figures were some of the most disorienting times I've ever been through. Knowing I'd just spent enough on a dress to feed a small country proved a mixed blessing at best.

Similarly, if it's you who have been disengaged, by whatever means and methods, you need to let yourself be cut loose, to practice what John Keats praised Shakespeare for possessing in such abundance: "negative capability . . . the capacity to be in mystery and doubt without any irritable searching after fact and reason." There are powerful pulls to do otherwise, to jump back into the game, to refill a schedule that has suddenly been emptied out, to seize at the first thing that would help pull you out of the mystery and doubt you will almost certainly be feeling by now in such abundance. But some things are meant to be, and this is one of them. Discomfort is more than okay — it's inevitable. The important thing is not to chicken out. Staying power counts here, maybe more than anywhere else. As Rosabeth Moss Kanter writes in *Evolve!*, "In the middle . . . perseverance of a change master . . . makes the difference between success and failure."

At best, there can be a heady sense of joy to this disengagement experience. Donald Marrs tells of being "light-headed as I moved through the halls, feeling what Alan Watts called a 'vacation experience,' the feeling of heightened release that comes from leaving all responsibility behind and heading for the open road." A "vacation experience"! You don't know the language. You're not sure what you've just ordered from the menu or if the water is safe to drink. But if you're going to enjoy the experience, you have to give yourself over to this differentness.

More often, there's a vulnerability, a sense of exposure that can be almost physically frightening. Bill Bridges talks about his own transition out of teaching in the early 1970s in stunning terms: "I had cast off the shell of my old identity like a lobster, and I was staying close to the rocks because I was still soft and vulnerable—I'd have a new and better identity in time, but for now I would have to go a little slowly."

What you have to remember is that you're doing hard work even when you seem to be doing nothing. You're shedding an old skin, the shell you've lived inside, the old way of knowing yourself and letting others know you. The finances might well be pinched, maybe badly strained, but if you can withstand the pain, the straining can be worth it many times over. This is not, nor can it be, a casual journey if it's going to come out right. This is a causal trip, instead, and a determinant one. And to the extent that you can, it deserves to be treated that way.

One way to survive this process of disengagement is to fall back on your essential nature: the hobbies, predilections, even the vices that can keep you going for a while. Some people drink a little more; some play a little more golf. It's likely to be years before you have this much time this empty again. The father of a former colleague eased across the gap between work and retirement by reading all of Charles Dickens's novels. When he finished and found he still wasn't ready to put on a new skin, he read all of Anthony Trollope. Then he became a full-time volunteer at his county historical society. I went a bit more lowbrow in my latest quest for amnesia: four candy bars a day, four hours of Tivo at night—prechosen, recorded programming of no redeeming social value that I could (and did) watch whenever I got home, even if that meant the TV was running at three in the morning.

If it feels good, do it. TV, trash novels, shopping, candy bars, an extra glass of wine, 27 holes of golf on a Wednesday—for the time being, escapism is a required part of the program.

During one of her gap crossings, Nancy Evans painted every stair of her four-story brownstone. Nancy is unusually productive by nature, so even her escapism involves productive activity. The closest I ever came to anything nearly so ambitious during one of these periods was rearranging my closet to absolute perfection at three in the morning: light to dark, color families grouped together. In another time of my life, I might have thought of such an exercise as marking a life without much substance, but I know I have a big life. It was just all the substance I could handle at the moment.

Yet another friend tells of taking two weeks off from his job in preparation for cancer surgery—another kind of gap crossing from what can be thought of as medical innocence to mortal experience. He had visions, he says, of getting his life in order, just in case. Instead, on his first morning home, he walked out into his yard, found a likely spot in the back corner just behind an apple tree, and called the local lumberyard with an order for enough cinder blocks, two-by-sixes, two-by-fours, siding, and hinges to build a first-rate shed, plus 10 or so pounds worth of galvanized nails and some clear corrugated plastic for the roof. On the day before he left for the hospital, he screwed down the last sheet of roofing and daubed the screw heads with caulk. There hasn't been a drop of rain inside the shed in the seven years since, he says.

It is by such small steps, however inspired, taken in whatever direction, that we occupy ourselves while the internal processes that will lead to reinvention begin.

Who Am I?

Letting loose of the external references of your life is hard work. In the whale's belly, there's no way to tell north from south, day from night. Letting go of your identity—disidentification—can be harder still.

There's a wonderful scene early on in the 1991 movie *City Slickers* where Billy Crystal—bored by his job as a radio ad salesman and depressed over turning 40—breaks down in tears in front of his son's elementary school class as he tries to explain just what he does for a living. Mitch Robbins, the character played by Crystal, doesn't know it yet, but he has already embarked on the comic journey of discovery that will take up the bulk of the film. Donald Justice's poem "The Missing Person" has a similar and haunting moment when a man walks into a police station to report himself missing, a poetic externalization of an internal process that will be familiar to many readers, especially those who have recently been through this falling stage themselves.

Part of the problem is that, in our culture, you often are what you do. Leave your job—even announce to the world that you are going to leave it—and you are leaving behind more than a title and a paycheck. You're abandoning an important part of your own self-definition, whether you defined yourself by the power you wielded, the friends you lunched and schmoozed with, the times your name could be found on hotbot.com or Lexis-Nexis, or the daily duties you performed and challenges you faced.

Another part of the problem is just the reverse: As you abandon your old life, your old life begins to abandon you. Friends will drop away, even people you thought were among your boon companions. This is as certain as death and taxes, and just as painful as both, and the more prepared you are for it going in, the better your chances of survival coming out the other side. Carole Hyatt and Linda Gottlieb, who wrote a classic on this subject, report that nearly every one of the 176 people they studied "were shocked at the number of friends who deserted them."

Again, no matter how we get to this point, the sense of disidentification, of abandonment, is likely to be just as powerful. There's always a touch of the leper to whoever leaves the pack. When we step outside an institution, we step outside a shared view of reality. The gossip base might still be the same—lunch is still possible—but our level of commitment to the dirt that's dished is no longer what it was. When the check has been paid and the tip calculated, our lunch partners will return to the old shared dream. We get to go somewhere else. By extension, our departure from the organization also suggests there is another reality available that lies outside the one everyone inside has been following. For the true believer, this disruption of the story line may be the hardest blow of all.

One friend was stunned when close associates—people he had worked side by side with for a dozen years—failed to even acknowledge that he was leaving the organization and then failed more overtly to make the effort to attend a going-away party. Finally, his wife cleared the matter up for him. All the reasons that had impelled him to go—an arid corporate culture, a lack of imagination and passion at the top, a desire to let his own creativity flourish somewhere where the soil and air were more nurturing—applied equally to many of his colleagues. They had been bitching and moaning about conditions together for nearly the whole time he had been there. Now he had the balls to actually leave, and they did not. Wouldn't you be a little sore under the circumstances, she asked? Wouldn't you feel as though you had been left in the lurch?

I had thought my own relationship with Nancy Evans was bombproof. We had been each other's backbone, support, and best friends for so many years. We had shared summer houses, plotted new businesses, dreamed and sweated until we finally stood together in the trading room at Goldman Sachs and watched our ticker symbol—IVIL—flash across the ticker for the very first time. On the wall of my new townhouse office, just over the top of the table where I do most of my work, there's a photo of the two of us fighting over French fries in a diner. Yet as I write, Nancy and I haven't spoken in nine months.

For weeks I didn't understand. We had always promised to leave together. In fact, when Nancy once fell afoul of the iVillage board and the directors were urging me to fire her, I'd told them that we were a package deal: If she went, I did. Now that I had pulled the ripcord and she hadn't, silence. And then it came to me that I had crossed into a reality that beckoned Nancy but that, for whatever reasons, she wasn't ready to share, and it had become too difficult for her to bridge the two realities.

One way to deal with this absence of a set identity is to borrow one, if only for a short while. Have business cards printed up, even if they show nothing but your name, mailing address, phone and fax numbers, and e-mail address. You'll have something to hand out when other people's cards start flying around the room. Just as important, you'll have something to consult in those existential moments when you're ready, like the Donald Justice poem, to declare yourself a missing person. More than one G.I. lost in the jungle or quavering in a foxhole has been heartened beyond words by a simple stamped-metal dogtag. If business cards aren't a part of your reality—and in this change-driven world, I think they'll be less and less a part of everyone's reality—you can always try the direct approach at these moments of introduction: "Oh hi, I'm John, and I'm unemployed." Taking full possession of what you are can be very powerful.

My friend Karen Quinn, who got the ax at American Express, has been busying herself designing a new company. I feel certain now that the company will become a success, but I told Karen early on that it didn't really matter if she moved to launch or not: What she was doing was the professional equivalent of needlepoint, a temporary identity that might or might not have any particular relation to what she next becomes. In a previous transition, I loaned myself out as a consultant at this relatively early stage—the idea mentioned earlier of renting the brain while holding on to the heart and passion. In 1994, to fill the gap between Q2 and iVillage, I did consulting for Ted Leonsis and Steve Case at America Online and for John Hendricks at the Discovery Network. Like Barry Diller, they were pioneers of new-media entrepreneurship, tutorials for my next life but no substitute for the life itself. This time around I shopped until I had no space left in my closet. By the time I was through, the doorman at the Versace shop on Fifth Avenue knew my name. "Hello, Ms. Carpenter," he would say as I arrived. "How are you today?" Oh, my God, I would think, what am I doing? But it didn't stop me from walking inside. Certainly, the shopping was a less cost-effective way of reminding myself who I am but, for me, just as effective in this circumstance as consulting had been in the last one. Things are building below the surface. Let them.

Even Craig Cohon, who knew with such absolute and complete certainty that his corporate executive chapter had ended and his new chapter as a philanthropic entrepreneur was about to begin, couldn't make the leap all at once. To give himself time to shed his old skin and get ready to put on his new one, Cohon signed on for six months to help a friend produce the 2001 World Economic Forum. He would quit before the six months were up, finally convinced that he was just killing time, just borrowing an ID to fight this sensation of falling out of time and place, but until that moment, his identity, too, needed a middle ground, a soft landing spot.

Another thing I've learned to do at this stage is to begin sorting through the lists of my friends and acquaintances. There's important work to be done here, too. Chapters accumulate people, and the higher you've gone, the wider the net you've cast in any one chapter, the more people will be piled up in your Rolodex at the end of it. A few months out of my daily duties at iVillage, I realized that I was supporting a series of Rolodexes with something on the order of 3,000 names in them — 3,000 people who, if they wouldn't call me a friend, would be certain to return my call within 24 hours if they could. It was simply too many people to carry forward.

Some people were obviously ripe for pruning. I had been the CEO of an Internet start-up, and in that role, there had been some real connection. Now my construct had changed, and theirs quite possibly, too. Outside of that work life, I couldn't imagine what we might talk about or meet on. Others pruned themselves. Not long after the Nasdaq crash of April 2000 I'd left the company, and I was at a fancy party in Manhattan when I saw two women across the room who had been bosom buddies of mine back when my paper worth, at least, was tripping over into the nine figures. By the time I'd worked my way across the room, it was clear they were heading for the door to avoid me. Fine, that was then; I was poorer now; and besides, I might not have made the best decisions when I was flying high about whom I would spend my time with. But off with their heads all the same! Or out with their index cards.

At the same time I was sorting out, I also began to sort in. Who were the 100 people among these 3,000 I would be physically pained by losing contact with? Who were the 25 within those 100 whom I couldn't live without? There are hard times in life, times when all the tea in China wouldn't be worth a single close and caring friend. However unsettled you might be in this period of falling, you can't let yourself lose sight of that. Nothing matters more than those we keep close to us. We remember best the ones who watch over us at these times.

What Was I?

The hard work hasn't ended. As our disidentification mounts, a sense of disenchantment is likely to settle in. The world you are moving away from seems less real; certain things you bought into then are simply not right. In truth, serial living can make this phase even worse: The more fully you are able to live in each chapter of your life, the more you are likely to buy into its sustaining stories and legends, and the more you do that, the more you will have left to untangle and sort through when you leave. Deep down, you're beginning to assemble the raw material out of which you will reframe the history of your own life. In this time of falling, it's a story that refuses to stand still.

Every organization tells myths about itself. Every great company builds up a history, a corporate culture that is in many ways the sum total of those myths. At the Walt Disney Corporation, it's taken as truth that desperate mothers and fathers abandon their children inside Disney theme parks in record numbers because they know the children will be safe there, taken care of, seen to. Is the story true? Who knows? But the story goes to the best of what Walt Disney employees want to believe about themselves and the organization they work for, which makes it true enough. To believe in Disney is to believe in it.

Coca-Cola didn't become the first and still the greatest global brand because its sugar-flavored, gas-laced water is necessarily better than anyone else's sugar-flavored, gas-laced water. It became the first and greatest through brilliant marketing and a corporate culture built around former chairman Robert Woodruff that wouldn't allow for anything less than firstness and greatness.

Early on in his tenure, so the story goes, Woodruff confronted the manager of a bottling plant who complained about new requirements that the equipment be cleaned daily. "It's just going to get dirty again," the manager told the new chairman. Woodruff, in turn, fixed him with a steely glance, rolled his cigar once across his mouth, and answered, "You wipe your ass, don't you?" True? Any truer than the story that Woodruff never allowed the word "Pepsi" to cross his lips? Any truer for that matter than the story that when Woodruff was dying, long after he'd given up his post, then chairman Robert Goizueta came to his home to get his blessing for a product the company was about to launch? "Do it," Woodruff is said to have finally rasped, his eyes brimming with tears, after which he refused all food and drink and thus was safely in his grave before the new New Coke went up in flames.

What's important in these stories isn't veracity—the Woodruff stories have been so retailed that they are de facto true in any event, if not de jure so. What's important is subscription. Great salespersons aren't delusional, as they so often can seem. The truly great ones have simply subscribed with every ounce of their belief into the sustaining myths of the products they are called upon to sell.

The same is true of great CEOs. Even if they don't lie at the heart of the corporate myth, they're still the embodiment of the story the company tells itself about itself. Like the chief of some primitive sub-Saharan tribe, they're not allowed to lie down lest the winds blow the village away. As Katherine Legatos found out, that can be the hardest duty of all when the winds start to howl.

John O'Neil, the author of *The Paradox of Success*, talked powerfully about this imperative of sustaining the history of the company even in the hardest of times—and by extension the history of its leader—when I talked with him in San Francisco.

"The one thing that most CEOs don't want to talk about is death," O'Neil told me. "They don't want to talk about the death of the company or the fact that it may have to become something different to survive. For that to happen, they'll have to give something up. Something is going to die for something to be born, and they don't want to discuss that.

"They're terrified of getting out of control, which is a very real fear when you've got so many demands. And they're afraid of their own mortality. They've fed themselves a dream that if only they are successful, then everything will be fine. Life will be good. We'll be able to make our wonderful choices. We'll be able to fulfill all of our childhood fantasies. The truth—and this is the paradox of success—is that success comes at a price, a big, big price.

"The final thing is that they carry everybody else's projections around, and they don't realize how heavy a burden that is. There's always someone saying, 'I want you to succeed because I'm a woman and I look to you as a role model.' Or 'I'm a shareholder, and I don't want to hear about your weakness. I want to hear that you're just about making money.' Or 'I'm a new hire here, and I want you to be gigantically successful so these little options I've got are going to turn into gold.'"

The problem with all that is that even if the company doesn't die, leaders themselves have a way of slipping out of the plot. When that happens, the task of supporting it, of playing your appointed role, becomes doubly difficult. From the outside, no corporate myth is as convincing as it is from deep within.

At iVillage we believed that we had found a better way on the Internet—a way to fill a huge niche with a happy marriage of advertisers, audience, enormous information resources, and a simple homespun utility that made things so very large seem so very small and intimate. I believed that absolutely then because I had to—belief like that starts at the top. I further believed absolutely that the stock market ultimately could not ignore the beauty of our concept and the obvious successes it was headed for. What's more, I believed both those things because I really believed them.

In the Zone, the story is all-important, all controlling, everything. Maybe if I could have stepped out of my skin then and had a look around, I would have seen that our stock—and indeed our entire industry sector—was in for a rough ride. But that's the whole point: In the heart of the Zone, there's a momentum, a forward motion as powerful as a tidal wave that positively won't allow you to step away. You've got to buy into the movement, got to be in the story, got to go with it all the way.

Do I still believe everything about iVillage that I believed then? Of course, but at some point as we step away, messianic zeal yields to simple conviction, a difference in degree though not in kind. Finally, in some deep level of his being, Robert Woodruff must have realized that the magical beverage he believed so fervently in was only bubbly, sugary colored water. Finally, too, as I moved away from iVillage, I had to admit to myself that what I would have sworn three years earlier was the Internet equivalent of the Second Coming was, after all, just a company, even if a terrific one.

What's the challenge in this phase of disenchantment? Not to succumb to cynicism, but to deepen our understanding and interpretation of the times we have just been through. Not to throw out our own history, but to revisit it with the knowledge we now have and to rewrite it in the light of what we now know. This is the chance to lay aside the blinding attachments that held us in our past and to listen carefully—as we never can when we're fully engaged—to the conversation that has been going on within ourselves about these things. More open to interpretation and less bound to old story lines, we can learn important things for going forward at the same time that we can still appreciate where we have been.

To be disenchanted requires, after all, that you first have the blessing of enchantment. Disillusionment simply asks us to reject our past altogether. Between the two points of view is a chasm as wide as the one you are leaping over.

Why Am I?

Disengaged, disidentified, and disenchanted, we fall into disorientation. Whether by our own hand or by someone else's, we've been disenfranchised, left without a vote in the world that used to matter so much to us. Whoever or whatever has pulled the plug, we've also been disempowered, cut off from a business or professional life—or even a personal one—from which we had so long drawn our strength and energy. I think, therefore I am, Descartes's famous dictum goes, but what if

Descartes had suddenly been disallowed from doing so? That's where we are: I am an executive, therefore I am. I am an entrepreneur, therefore I am. I am a teacher, therefore I am. I am a stay-at-home mom, therefore I am. No more.

Valerie Salembier had been president of the *New York Post*—a job she loved and one she had worked her way up to through many years of hard work—when one day, out of the blue, she was fired. Two months later, after going through a storm of emotions, Valerie was scheduled to attend a gathering of women executives. In her old job, she wouldn't have hesitated for a second. Now she literally got on and off the plane four times before finally settling into her seat. At the meeting, the women went around the room, telling who they were. When Valerie's turn came, all she could think to say was, "I'm Valerie. I'm the newly fired president of the *New York Post*." Everyone laughed and fell in love with her, Valerie said, but her pain was still there and abundantly real.

When I walked away from iVillage, I had been a leader of people for a quarter century—from mountain expeditions to ever-larger corporate teams to, finally, my very own entrepreneurial dream. Leading was what I did, who I was, why I was; yet suddenly there was no one other than my two little girls to follow me. (And little girls, as is well known, have very strong minds of their own.) A general without troops, I lost any motive, drive, or even good reason so far as I could see to ever exercise command again. At some point in this process, I happened to have lunch with Tom O'Leary, a former Jesuit priest who helps people organize their lives at these moments. I was already at the table when Tom came into the restaurant, so it wasn't until we stood up at the end of the meal that he got a full look at me.

"Oh, my God," I remember his saying. "You're about two inches taller than I thought you were. The things you talked about made you seem much softer and more fragile."

He was right, too. There's a loss of faith that comes with this disorientation and that feeds it in equal measure. I knew I'd get through these painful consequences of a change I so much wanted to make. I've always found this period to be self-limiting and self-correcting, and it was. Six months later I emerged on the other side of my disorientation with a far deeper understanding of the conditions in which I enjoy leading. Valerie Salembier triumphed, too, going on to become SVP and publisher of *Family Circle* and VP and publisher of *Esquire*. But faith in the outcome is weak solace at the moment.

The "disses" in our lives are mounting, dislocating us in both a physical and spiritual sense, cutting us off from our own deeper meaning and calling. In a sense nothing could be more necessary: We have to disintegrate before we can be reintegrated, come unglued before we can glue ourselves back together, let our reality come apart completely so that we won't repeat it mindlessly. But even that knowledge is slim reassurance when parts of our self-understanding are flying off in all directions and we seem to have lost sight of our essential being. In time we'll see all this for what it is: a symbolic destruction that is really a new beginning. But getting from here to there can be awful.

Nancy Evans describes this as the living-in-Kansas period, a wonderfully apt phrase when you happen to be living on Manhattan Island. Fired from her job running a major publishing house in one of those political shake-ups that periodically sweep through the book industry, Nancy went in a matter almost of days from being a staple of the gossip writers to near oblivion. To cope with her sense of disorientation, Nancy started each morning by making a list of what a mother in Kansas might do that day. Checking the gossip columns to see if her name was there and lunching at the Four Seasons were not even low priorities in the life she imagined for herself. If nothing else, "living in Kansas" gives you a place to go in your own head until you're ready to move forward. If you happen to live in Manhattan, Kansas, try thinking of this as your living-on-Manhattan-Island period. The effect should be the same.

Randy Christofferson had been president of First USA bank when it was sold to BankOne. By any reasonable standard, he never needs to work again. Yet Randy told me not long ago that he has a recurring dream in which he has done the math wrong. He's in his mid-fifties in his dream, he said, in desperate need of going back to work, but he has dropped completely off the business world radar screen. So vivid was the dream that Randy for a time started a little company, just to keep himself in the game. Not until he realized that he no longer cared about this game could Randy let the company and the recurring dream go.

Carole Hyatt and Linda Gottlieb suggest performing a kind of practical triage at this point. Find someone you trust, and tell him or her out loud the things you most fear: I'll run out of money. People will think I've taken the easy way out. I've abandoned my troops. I'll never live in such a nice neighborhood again. I've fallen permanently below the radar. My parents/siblings/spouse/child(ren) will think I've failed. Whatever it is, confront it and realize that it won't kill you even if the worst case should come to pass. Chances are you're still looking at the issue from the perspective of the world you're leaving—it is, after all, the only fully formed perspective you've known in some time, even if it is breaking up in front of your eyes. But what seems a death in life in one chapter can be the beginning of life and wisdom in another.

This can be a good time, too, to deal with other emotions—not to relive the past so much as to extract what wisdom you can from the pain you suffered. (For all the agony they cause, abscessed teeth and gums do tend to lead us to better oral hygiene.) What are you angry about from your past chapter? Most saddened by? Most regretful of? What would you have done differently? What experiences do you want to carry forward into your new life? The point is never to punish yourself. It's to learn. Honestly confronting such questions will begin to tell you what you want to avoid or embrace in the life you are headed to. Avoiding the questions and underlying issues is an invitation to repeating the same mistakes.

A good friend tells the story of an executive she hired who had been done in, so he felt, by a cabal of women at his previous stop, a major Fortune 100 corporation. "The first time we had a disagreement with him," she told me, "he lashed out at us. I couldn't understand it—it was completely irrational and out of proportion to the incident—and then I realized he was still angry at the women at his old place. He was playing a game of vindication, not creation."

Ted Waite found a far better solution. Ted loved creating Gateway from scratch in his garage, but he hated being rich. To resolve the dilemma and reground himself, he formed the Foundation for the Future and hired a good friend to help him get rid of the money that was making him miserable.

As the iVillage stock price unwound, the financial analysts who follow and track these things kept harping on me and my leopard glasses. I found myself enraged. They were nothing more than a variation on basic horn-rims. But the more I examined my anger—the more I peeled back its layers and held them all up to the light— the more I realized that what was really at issue was the ambivalence about power and femininity, and that I wanted nothing more to do with the subject or with a job that forced me to play "boy." An extraordinarily useful lesson, however painfully won, and a truth that has helped set me free.

Money

At a more basic level, going through this methodical process of confronting fear will help you cope with the free-floating anxiety so common to periods of disorientation. The understandings you arrive at might not be big ones, but you're not baking the bread of your next life yet; you're just assembling the ingredients. Even if you're financially secure by all objective measures, fears about money are going to be a staple of this phase. You've come unmoored from your own sense of self. Without some kind of solid financial plan in place, you're likely to continue drifting, latching on to short-term solutions when what you really need is a strategy that serves the long-term goal of reinvention.

At the most basic level, you can simply take your total reserve, subtract from that the reserve you don't want to touch, and divide the resulting figure by your monthly expenses. Once you know how many months—or weeks—you can afford, you'll need to augment the math by factoring in your own capacities and needs, and by hard choices. How much supplemental income can you earn without giving your heart away?

A cocktail napkin will serve just fine. Take your cash reserves, subtract the minimum you need to keep back to feel safe, and divide what's left by your monthly fixed costs. That's how long you have to reinvent yourself.

What can you do without in the short term that might stretch three months to six? Six to nine? What are the security blankets that you just can't jettison? Finally, the cold math of such financial planning becomes intensely personal.

Michelle Smith, who specializes in financial advice to people in transition, told me about two clients she had recently worked with. One quit on the spot, didn't cut back on her living expenses in the least, and within nine months her new business had grossed $10 million. The other cut her costs to the bone within a week after saying goodbye to her old job, even selling a second home. In consequence, she had bought up to three years to discover what her next chapter would be. One friend harbors a secret fantasy of retiring early from his stressful media job, selling his large suburban house in favor of a cheaper in-town condo, and using the profit from the sale to support himself while he spends five to ten years teaching adult literacy. I think he'll do it, not just because he has been thinking carefully about the finances but because he has the passion and determination that are necessary to carry through the hard choices of reinvention.

I've known Betsy since elementary school. The "best" job she ever held was as an assistant children's librarian in the small New England town where she now lives. Between her two husbands, she and her two children were on food stamps for half a year. Not long after she remarried, an auto wreck nearly killed her. For two years, she had virtually no use of her left leg. That's the downside of Betsy's life. The upside is that she happens to love books and children, and the years she spent as an assistant librarian were among the happiest of her life. Her husband has been semiretired since his early fifties. He takes long-term substitute teaching jobs at the local high school. On collective annual earnings that couldn't exceed $40,000, the two of them have seen more of the world than I have. Betsy's Marine Corps son has been stationed at embassies throughout northern Africa and the Middle East, and she has been to visit him at every stop. Her hotels are two stars, not five. She takes the last-minute cheap seats on planes and wears out a lot of shoe leather instead of renting cars. But she goes and does and lives fully in the moment of each event. We were sitting on the front porch of their small clapboard house not long ago when Betsy told me that she has always thought of her life as a process of becoming. "If I had thought I was going to be on food stamps for the rest of my life, I honestly think I would have packed it in," she said. "But I kept telling myself that we were going to get to the end of this bad time, and when we did, something interesting would be waiting for us. And it has been waiting there, always." Once we get the conversation right in our own heads, the money has a way of falling into line.

If you don't like how the numbers came out the first time, what can you change in your life to extend the time available for self-discovery?

When I stepped down as CEO of iVillage, I was determined to carve out a year to write, think, and teach, but I also decided not to alter my lifestyle dramatically because I was already absorbing as much change as I could handle. Instead, I would supplement my income by taking on speaking engagements and by consulting. If the necessary infrastructure hasn't begun to build within six months, I'll rethink the matter, I told myself, but until then, I'm sticking with the plan. And that's just what I've done. Another person, faced with the same set of facts, might well have decided to cut back immediately, but that's her, not me. One thing you have to be through all of this is true to yourself. When it's another life you are creating, you can't use a store-bought mix. This bread has to be made from scratch.

The Art of Navigation

All of this hard work can be helped immensely by the services of what I've come to think of as the Navigator, someone who can help guide you through this process but who retains no stake in its outcome. That's not the same as a trusted friend or a spouse. The people we trust most, indeed, tend to have the greatest stakes in our outcome. The wife of an investment banker is apt to have to make serious and sudden sacrifices if he is to fulfill his desire to give up high finance for abstract painting. Your business partner will have to retool if you leave. Your best friend might take pride in your success or fear that she'll have to bear an inordinate amount of the pain you'll suffer in any prolonged transition. Or she might just think it would be cool to have a best friend of her own who gave it all up to write novels or who grabbed the CEO slot at Lazard Frères when all his silent signs were telling him to do otherwise.

New York City is not a normal place to live. In most other cities, drivers are a luxury for the very rich or the very pretentious. Here, they are for the very exhausted. One friend swears he would eat peanut butter and jelly sandwiches for an entire year if necessary to keep his driver. My own driver is an inordinately wise man—a Russian émigré who was a physician before geopolitics ripped his old chapter apart. But wise as he is, he had known me only as one thing—a corporate CEO. When he started dropping me off at my girls' schools, Versace, and church in no particular order, instead of the office, he was convinced the end was near. His view of me was not large enough to embrace another life for me. I think Nancy Evans and I went astray over this matter of Navigators, too. We were still using each other as life guides even after iVillage had created such an organic connection between us that the actions of one had no choice but to affect the life of the other. Like Siamese twins, we were sharing bones, organs, tissue—not the best situation for independent judgments.

A Navigator has to be someone who admires you and is confident in your ability to make anything you want happen. Just as a Navigator can't have a stake in chaining you to your past, so he or she should not artificially limit your future by prejudging your capacities. This isn't a career aptitude test you're taking; it's the first steps of an enormous journey. A Navigator who starts in on you about the mistakes you've made to get to this point is the wrong person for the job. So is a Navigator who tells you to take the first job you're offered because doing so would tidy up your life. In all likelihood, such a guide is also trying to rid herself of the discomfort of dealing with you in this vulnerable state. And a Navigator— a good one—also won't start out by insisting you fix what has to come undone before it can be put back together again. Letting yourself get thoroughly broken open is a large part of the idea here.

A Navigator's job is to understand the cycle you're passing through, have a map filled not with specific destinations but with infinite possibilities, breathe the air you are breathing so she knows when to leave you alone for weeks at a time if necessary and when to attend to you every day, and through it all to project total confidence in your capacity to get from where you've been to where you're going, even when you yourself are still feeling as if you've fallen into a deep canyon along the way. If ever a job called for self-abnegation, for dis-appearing into one's duties, it is this one: "Like a bridge over troubled waters," in Simon and Garfunkel's beautiful anthem, "I will lay me down."

In effect, a Navigator is a short-term therapist, but what he is asked to do comes as readily out of the arts as it does out of the therapeutic tradition. Like a novelist at page one, a painter facing an empty canvas, or a composer before an unscored sheet, you are embarking on an act of personal cre-ation. The first word tells you the second one, the second the third, as each of the words begins to build plot, character, tone, style. With each brush stroke, the painting both defines and redefines itself. A note becomes a chord; chords create movements; movements make symphonies. The Navigator has to understand that, and has to understand that every one of those words, those daubs of paint, those flats and sharps, majors and minors, has to come ultimately from within you.

A pastor can be useful here, or a trusted friend with no vested interest in the outcome. What you're really looking for is a wise person, whatever the specific background or credentials. If no one comes to mind and you'd like a referral to one of the new breed of what are called "transition coaches," call the Transitions Institute at (214) 528-9401.

Find a Navigator to help show you the way. You'll need someone who thinks you can do anything and has no investment in what you have been. Your spouse or best friend is likely to volunteer, but does he or she fit the criteria?

I signed up with several transition coaches even though one would have been enough, because I was learning for more than myself, and all have helped form the foundation of wisdom that I've tried to build this book on. My guess is that transition coaching will become one of the great boutique professions of the next two decades. As more and more of us move toward serial lives, as we recognize that we can live our lives chapter by chapter, not all a jumble at once, the demand and need for Navigators will grow and grow, especially among men in transition.

Carole Hyatt and Linda Gottlieb found in their research that nine in ten men kept their own counsel rather than confide in someone about the difficulties of letting go of an old life and reaching out to a new one. Little is the surprise, of course. Successful, hard-driving people generally do not like sharing a sense of disorientation. But men not only lack the stomach for it; they don't always have a vocabulary that would allow them to share. Nor are hard-driving people comfortable with discussing all the confusing emotions and thoughts that are so critical to a successful passage from past to future.

I'm convinced, though, that we can and must change that conversational capacity. I'm convinced that once we build a belief system around the legitimacy of these transitions, the words to talk about them will follow. Divorce was once a taboo subject. Death was once greeted with silence. Today, we can talk freely about both of them because we have the language for it. Tomorrow, we'll have the language for this. Not long ago, I was talking with a close friend and business associate about his former career in advertising. He had worked his way to near the top of a small, well-regarded agency. When a recession hit and revenues went into sharp decline, he tried to talk the owner into merging with a larger agency. When she gave a definitive no to his idea, he walked away from his job and the agency over lunch.

"I said, 'That's it. I'm out of here.' I got a bottle of vodka, took my girlfriend home, and we got wildly drunk. I went back to the agency at midnight, carried out every vestige of my past life, and never went back into the building again. Then I fell and fell. It was six months before I was on my feet again, six months of spinning, of wondering 'Where am I?,' of drugs and alcohol. The altered state had taken over. Finally, reality intervened in the form of a one-year-old child, and I said 'enough already.' But it was a major, major fall."

His pain was visible as he talked, his own pain and the pain he had inflicted on others. You could feel all those lost months of life, just as if they were sitting in the room with us. I felt for him, to be sure, but I also couldn't help but think: This conversation is progress. This is the vanguard of great change.

CHAPTER FOUR

A Walk in the Desert

The wilderness and the solitary place shall be glad for them; and the desert shall rejoice, and blossom as a rose.

—Book of Isaiah

I'm not sure exactly when it happened—time blurs in these in-between periods—but one day I realized that I was no longer rushing home to my nightly pile-up of taped TV shows. The four candy bars a day were gone; I'd stopped organizing, and reorganizing, my closet. The Versace doorman probably forgot my name as quickly as he had learned it. Instead of Tivo, I found myself once again drawn to books. I began reading avidly and taking long walks. For more than half a year I had held on to the title of chairman of iVillage as a treasured identity. Now I dropped it, and I turned my cell phone off, too, for hours at a time. I realized that I was too engaged in simply being to let in many distractions from the outside world, and that's when I knew for sure that my falling was over.

When you begin to feel this return to center, you've made it to the other side, to the "no-place" where anything is still possible and nothing is yet chosen. I like the image of the desert for this spot you've come to: There's nothing to impede you. You can see almost forever in almost any direction. Sandstorms may come up. You'll need to keep an eye on where the oasis is, and you'll have to be conscious of the shifting dunes—landmarks in the desert are inherently unstable. But all it takes is a little rain for the floor beneath your feet to burst into the most remarkable array of blossoms. There's no joy in falling. Here, joy is all around you.

Although you still have no set identity, you're now gathering the materials that will lead you to that person-to-be. You also should be far more comfortable with not knowing precisely who you are and what your future holds. If you had a business card made up earlier, it was likely to serve more as a safe harbor from the existential storm. You don't need the card now. The uncertainty of your life holds more promise than peril.

You're still likely to have a powerful sense of aloneness, too, but you can relish it now. In the quiet, on this neutral ground, you'll be discovering the unique sequences and codings of personality that make you what you are and that spell a large part of your professional destiny. This is among the most serious work you will ever do—work that requires solitude and needs time.

At the start of this journey, in the solitude of the desert, you are also likely to hear powerful voices calling you from what is now the far side of the chasm. It's not until you've crossed over—gotten through the disorientation of falling—that you really have time to stop and think with anything approaching clarity about what you have left behind.

When I left my mountaineering chapter for a corporate one, I knew I was changing the terms of my life, but until I ended up in New York City without my husband, I had no idea how lonely loneliness can be. In the mountains, values had been built around collaboration, courage, and kindness; they had to be for survival's sake. At American Express as at any big corporation, the value set and survival skills were completely different. In Colorado and Wyoming, where I had spent the bulk of my time, the most important currency we were paid in was friendship. At American Express, rewards came in the form of raises, rank, and office space. And as has happened in every chapter transition since, I longed, sometimes desperately, to return to where I had come from. Now that I had left, the voices crying "Go back!" sometimes seemed deafening.

I listened to those voices as I was getting ready to start iVillage because I thought I had to. I was a single mother with plenty of obligations. I interviewed for a number of jobs that would have provided nicely for me and my tiny family. All I would have had to do was delay the full realization of my entrepreneurial chapter a few years longer. And after every interview, every single time, I walked into the nearest bathroom and threw up. I want to sell out, I told myself, but this body isn't going to let me.

> Don't act—wait. When invitations to walk back into your old life arrive, be flattered, but hold your ground. Something important is happening; you need to give it time to unfold.

When you're falling, time is both ally and enemy. Nobody in free fall ever wished to hit the ground sooner, but every moment in between can seem to drag on into eternity.

Once you land, time becomes a huge gift, unalloyed. If you can possibly afford it, give yourself a month, a year. Trust me, escape behaviors will fall away. You won't spend all that time you've bought so dearly in color-coordinating your wardrobe or building the perfect shed. There's too much at stake. If you can't afford full time—if the mortgage has to be paid or the college bills, new or old—do what we talked about: Rent yourself out; don't sell. There's a spaciousness to this no-place, an endless stretching in every direction that busy people never get to enjoy. The sacrifices you make now to allow you to live as fully as possible inside these rare moments will be repaid exponentially down the road.

My daughter likes school, but I'm still hard-pressed to get her out of bed by seven in the morning so she can get there. Last week, when she had a day off, Michaela popped out of bed at seven sharp and shouted, "No school!" That's where we have landed.

Randy Christofferson knows more than most of us about putting in 80- and 90-hour workweeks. He has been in the center of lots of business storms, including the dot-com storm, but when I talked with him not long ago at his home in Delaware, he was planning to do the grocery shopping for his wife and four children, and maybe slip in a nap before taking in one of his kid's lacrosse games. He had also just committed to coaching the school's hockey team for three years—five hours a day, five days a week, four months a year. He'll ride to the rink with the team on a yellow school bus, quite a change for someone who rode to his last job in a helicopter. The coaching commitment, he told me, was his own way of holding himself in this in-between space, a way to assure that he would keep busy with just being.

More than anything else, maybe, I was struck by how happy Randy seemed, but I'm always surprised to find how content I am in this desert, too. I hate the sensation of falling, hate the disorientation, but once I get to this moonscape, this stark expanse, I invariably start finding out new things about myself, about where my growth has taken me so far and where it might take me from here. And the more I'm able to avoid shortcuts, the more adamant I am about not saying yes to the temptations to jump back into the fight, the more complete my education is each time. So much of our life is about externals, about never letting anyone smell the fear. Here you can be vulnerable. Here you can go inside. In a sense, you're practicing zero-based budgeting. You've thrown everything nonessential out of your life, all the extraneous line items. Now they have to justify their way back in, one by one.

Donald Marrs describes this period in his life in language that will be familiar to anyone who has been there: "I had begun to open myself to feelings I hadn't had in a lifetime. It was as though a hard, grisly period had ended and a softer and more internal time had begun." Just as Nancy Evans's "mother-in-Kansas" strategy had synchronized her own life with the rhythms of her disorientation after she was fired, so Marrs's move from a Chicago high-rise to a glass house deep in a canyon in Santa Monica synchronized his life with this part of the journey he had set out on. When you're falling, almost no one wants to be alone; once you land, solitude can become an absolute craving. For companionship, Marrs had the deer that he startled on his morning walks.

My social schedule, once insanely packed, is down to time with my kids and a very small set of friends and family. I'm helping two new companies get off the ground and taking limited speaking engagements. That may already sound crowded, but the noise level in my life right now is about a tenth what it was. I can hear myself, hear what's stirring beneath and around me. At iVillage, almost all my fantasies involved naps—there was never enough time in the day, never. Now, I fantasize about hiking for days alone over mountain passes, the terrain I cut my teeth on just out of college but without the burden of leading a group. A great drama is forming in the wings, just out of sight in this stage; the more receptive we can make ourselves, the easier recognition and understanding will be once the drama reveals itself.

Forget goals for the moment. Give yourself over to the moment the way kids at play so often do. After all the years of striving, the feeling can be ecstatic. Besides, isn't a desert just a great big sandbox?

No one I know has used this time more effectively than Chris Ogden. Chris was working in the cable industry when he took off the first time, to spend three years in the Rocky Mountains and then sailing. The second time, now nearing the end of a divorce, he gave up a career packaging programming for public television, in what amounted to the second part of an epic spiritual quest that finally landed him on the West Coast, studying to be a therapist.

"The first time I was in Miami, and I guess one of the events that brought it about was the fact that I didn't need to take care of my son, Ian, any longer. He was old enough to take care of himself. That allowed me to look at the quality of my life. Now that I didn't have anyone depending on me, I could ask if I was enjoying myself, if I was feeling good about my work. When I looked at it, the obvious answer was, 'No. I don't like it. It's not fulfilling, and I don't want to do this.' And it was scary, very scary, because then I had to ask: 'Okay, if I don't do this, what do I do?'

"I had sessions with shrinks. I talked to people. I went through this whole frightened thing where I was like, 'If I'm not this, then who am I? If I don't do this, what am I going to do?' And through a lot of encouragement from a lot of different spaces, I finally took off and just spent three years doing whatever I felt like doing, which was hiking and skiing in Colorado and then sailing.

"And then virtually the same thing happened in the second experience. As the divorce was winding down, I again found myself in that space of saying, 'Okay. I have only me to be responsible for. There is no justification for doing something that doesn't fulfill me or that I don't like. If I'm still happy in it, great—then I should keep doing it. But if I'm not, then I should not do it.' I was far enough into the divorce that I could see the end of it coming and pretty much realized that, okay, this is going to be when I once again have a life that's really not determined by anything other than what I choose to do. And that's when I started to really look inside myself and say: 'What do I want my life to look like? What can I do to make it look like that?'

"I'd just taken the three years off a couple of years prior, so one of the things I knew was that I really didn't ever want to have to retire. I would never be comfortable in a golf-course community in Naples, Florida—I would get bored very quickly. So I realized that I wanted to do something that I could do until I was 85 if I chose to. I wanted that. When I looked back at my life, I also thought that my work had never been fulfilling. It had always been work that allowed me to meet responsibilities, not to fulfill my own inner needs or desires. I'd always put those on the back burner because I had Ian to take care of, or my marriage to see to, or whatever.

"As I started to look at that, I thought, well, what experiences have I had in my life that were fulfilling? Have I done anything, even if it was for a minute or a day, that was truly fulfilling? Was sailing? Should I be a boat captain? Maybe a charter captain? Should I teach riding? I really examined every experience in my life, and as I looked through that, the thing that I found had given me more feelings of fulfillment, of value, were the times that I spent working with alcoholics, sponsoring people, and watching their lives come together, at least partially because of my help. And that's what led me to say, 'Well, wouldn't it be great if I could do that—help people in that way and get paid for it? And instead of doing it without really knowing what the hell to do, do it well, get paid for it, and do it as much as I wanted for as long as I wanted?'"

It was that realization that began the separation from TV packaging that eventually left Chris Ogden a 50-year-old graduate student in a city he had never lived in before, in a field he held no credentials or had no previous experience in.

I realize this can sound like precious territory, but Chris was doing all this with no safety net. What he had instead of money was freedom from responsibility and the guts, the raw courage, to walk through the desert longer than most of us could stand. (Courage isn't to be sold short in any of this.) Chris also had the instinctive genius during the second half of his spiritual quest to turn the normal equation of such explorations on its ear. Rather than begin with the job, the position, the place, the external trappings of the new life he was headed to, he began with himself. Chris went back—maybe more accurately down—into himself; he became his own spelunker. And what he found in that cave at the center of his being was someone who wanted more than anything else to help people with the same addiction to alcohol that he suffered from. After that, he says, the answer to the questions he had been asking was unavoidable and compelling, however painful getting there still would be. Chris began to build his life from the inside out, not the outside in. That's an important part of what this walk in the desert is all about.

"I think that what made the difference is that instead of looking at all the jobs in the world and saying, 'Which one might be fun to do? A butcher? A baker? A candlestick maker?' I looked instead at my experience and said, 'What do I want my life to look like?' Once that had happened, once I went at it from that angle, it was very quick. I sat in my apartment in New York one Saturday afternoon, and I thought, 'Well, who do I want to be? How do I want the next 30 years of my life, if I live to be 87, to look?' And I just sort of fantasized. What would I want to do? How do I want to live? What do I want to be doing? What's been fulfilling for me in the past? As I filled in all those places in that questioning, the picture became self-obvious."

Enjoy the view. For the first time, you should be able to see clearly where you have been and the early outlines of whom you want to be when you grow up.

Goodbye to All That

The processes my transition coaches have taken me through have varied greatly one from the other: Some are more test-oriented; others more talk-oriented. The social sciences, psychology, psychiatry, and even spirituality work their way through everyone's work to a greater or lesser degree, but some coaches lean toward the vocabulary of the classroom, others toward that of the boardroom. The cost has varied greatly, too. The going rate has ranged from several hundred dollars to the $50,000 course at the Center for Creative Options that's usually reserved for CEOs hoping to redirect their always massive energies. Whichever advice route I followed, though—and they've all been extraordinarily worthwhile—all of the transition programs came down in the end to much the same thing.

Everyone agrees, for example, that this is a time to say goodbye to the past. In the falling stage, you might have taken time to recognize your emotions and think about their implications. You might even have had fleeting glimpses of where this wave of change was carrying you, but you weren't ready to let go of who you were. Now that you're safely across the chasm, you should be able to do that. Begin by breaking the literal ties that are holding you back. After I left iVillage, I kept the title of chairman even though I had given up any day-to-day responsibility for the company. When I gave up even that, I knew that I was moving forward for good, and I was shocked by the freedom and energy that was released by this simple shedding of what I thought had become a largely symbolic title. We carry weights we don't even know about until we put them down.

For other people, the ties are smaller but no less hobbling. One friend wore a baseball cap emblazoned with her old company's logo whenever she went jogging, for months after she no longer worked for the company. The cap fit, her head was used to it, and she looked good in it, she told me. It was only when she convinced herself that she was never going back to her old boss and never going to be the person who worked for him in that place that she could throw the cap away.

Once you've freed yourself physically from who you were, it's time to free yourself emotionally—harder work. Like Chris Ogden, you'll need to create a version of your own history that can guide you as you go forward, not protect the ego you've accumulated over all your past years. What's needed now is analysis and honesty, and a determination to learn from what might be painful discoveries.

Maybe your last gig began successfully and brought you great satisfaction, only to become less so on both fronts as the company grew bigger and more corporate in nature and customs. What have you learned if that's the case? That you thrive in chaos and wilt in a more controlled environment? That's an important lesson in general, but it also has specific applications: If you've been dreaming of being CEO of a Fortune 1000 company, you might be dreaming of the wrong position in the wrong place, at least for now.

Equally, you might discover on examination that the unpredictability of events in a new company is disabling to you. Your personality just doesn't run that way. The sum total of experiences that has made you what you are has outfitted you otherwise. The CFO we brought in at iVillage was so uncomfortable with the invisible bumps and slim margins for error in a start-up that I don't think he drew a relaxed breath in two and a half years. He was wired for certainty. There's no right or wrong here, just as there's no right or wrong in any scientific research properly done. You're looking for answers, not confirmations of possibly wrong suppositions about yourself. Not everyone belongs to the same degree in every environment.

Maybe you can now admit that you abandoned your family in your past job to an extent you don't want to duplicate in the next one. That realization comes hard, painfully for many of us, but better to learn it about yourself and your loved ones now than in 10 years when the damage may be irreparable. Maybe the years you spent being a consultant or a freelancer or a lone-wolf day trader left you feeling too far from the action, or the years you spent running the division or the dyeing mill or the corporate headquarters left you feeling like you never had enough privacy. Maybe you're tired of spending your time on paperwork rather than patients. These aren't casual messages. They're important imperatives of your own personality that need to be in balance if where you are headed is going to bring you the peace and happiness you supposedly are headed there to find. If your body told you that you suffered from adult-onset diabetes, you'd pay attention or face the peril. This is no different. You need to listen and realize what will happen if you don't.

The strongest reason I know for not jumping out of one major job into the next is precisely this: You need to be sure, as certain as you can be in an uncertain world, that you have learned as much as possible about where you thrive before you set out to thrive there. If the urge to leave is driven largely by burnout, say, unaccompanied by serious reflection on where and how your job has been most and least fulfilling, you're likely to simply repeat in your next situation all the conditions and situations you find so wearing in your current one.

Fritts Golden was a biology major at Swarthmore College when he got interested in environmental activism. After a post-college year at a job in Antarctica, he went on to graduate school in environmental planning. Straight out of graduate school, he and a partner started an environmental consultancy in Philadelphia that eventually swelled to 50 people.

"After we got started in Philadelphia, I opened a branch office down in Washington," Fritts told me. "As a child I had been brought up in foster care in California, and one of the things you learn in that situation very quickly is how to please people. I was a good schmoozer with clients, and Washington was a logical place to exercise my talent. I was down from Philadelphia to Baltimore or Washington nearly every week. After 15 years, we sold the business in 1990 to a very large international engineering firm, and I slipped from being one of the partners to being a senior person basically without a portfolio. Washington and Baltimore were in a different marketing region of the new firm, so I was cut off from that set of business contacts. I kicked around in the new organization in Philadelphia for a couple of years, through several reorganizations in the company. Then they asked me to come out to Oakland to run a department in the office there, so my wife, Kay, and I moved out here to California with our two kids."

The job, though, didn't pan out as hoped. The company redefined Fritts's role shortly after he arrived. To make matters worse, the local client base he would be most comfortable handling had already been divided up among the old hands. Not long after, he left it for a smaller environmental group. The fit would be better, he thought, and the size more in line with his personality. What he hadn't counted on was that a new president would come in and quickly whittle away his turf.

"After a frustrating year and a half I left by mutual agreement, and I took six months off to do some writing and to take a hard look at myself—what I wanted to do. What kind of person am I? What do I really like to do? I like to host things, I finally figured out. I like to make sure people are comfortable and entertained, and the host industry is the restaurant industry."

After a long search, Fritts and his wife bought a gourmet deli in tony Sausalito, across the Golden Gate Bridge from San Francisco. Their intent was for Fritts to turn it into a table restaurant that would cater to the business lunch crowd and the weekend brunch clientele, but like others before them, they quickly discovered the downside of the business: long, inflexible hours; high staff turnover; tight margins; fickle tastes. A little more than half a year into the restaurant trade, they knew they needed to get out. More than a year later, they were finally able to sell the deli.

"I was immediately invited into an independent consulting assignment," Fritts went on, "and I made more money in a month than I had in two years with the restaurant. Within two months, I had two firms asking me to work full time. Still, I got something out of the break. I realized that each step you take is a more mature step. You go back under your own terms. You say, 'here's what I want to do and how I can contribute and here's what I don't want to do.' What I realized was that it wasn't the environmental industry that was a problem. It was finding the right organization with the right people and the right mindset."

That kind of self-knowledge never comes easily or cheaply, but it shouldn't have to be so expensive in terms of time and money. On four or five occasions over six years at iVillage, clearly exhausted executives came to me and said they were leaving for another job. I was rarely surprised—four or five years of the Internet race was like wearing flippers to run a marathon; it consumed people—but in every case, I counseled the departing execs to take at least a few weeks off with their families to make sure they were going to the right place for the right reasons. And in over half those instances, the former employees called me within a month to say that they had mistaken burnout for disenchantment, were now stuck working even harder in a new situation, and were getting still more burned out as a result. A few of them even came back to iVillage, once they realized the dynamics at work in their lives. The work world is hard enough. It doesn't have to be top heavy with regret, too.

One more thing: In this period of analysis, where you are plumbing your past to understand your future, don't neglect what might seem like small things. This baseline work personality you are searching for has been manifesting itself your whole life and in ways that spill far beyond the workplace. What brought you the greatest satisfaction in college? In high school? What nonwork activities would it physically pain you to cut loose? I have a friend who's miserable in a day job that he happens nonetheless to be very good at and who finds enormous fulfillment in singing for a church choir that he can never find adequate time to devote to. If he were ever to ask me to be his Navigator, I would simply point this out to him: Our joys and our workdays don't have to be so far apart.

I remember so well sitting on a porch in the Adirondacks a few years back, listening to an old friend as he lamented the turns his life had taken: What he thought had been a true romance wasn't. Banking had provided well for him financially but had offered little spiritually. If he had it to do all over again, he said, he would have taken a degree in museum curating and devoted his workdays to the mountain crafts he so loved. He didn't care about the money, he told me; the crafts would give him meaning. So do it, I answered. You've just sent yourself the message; now listen to it. Capture it. Today, he's curator of a small, exquisite New England museum, happier than I've ever known him to be.

It was during this analytical process that my Navigator reminded me how much satisfaction I had drawn from chairing the prom committee in high school three decades earlier. Making sure the thousand feet of hand-drawn Rousseau murals were hung perfectly and the eyes of the 50-foot dragon were flashing intensely had brought me enormous satisfaction. So had the 2,000 stars hanging from nets in the ceiling and the island with water running under a real bridge. What does it mean? That I'm bossy? That I like a party? That I take pleasure in leading others toward common and daunting goals? That I like a little chaos in my life? I'm still not absolutely sure, but I intend to keep thinking about the matter. The clues about ourselves are all around us. We only have to open our eyes to find them.

Broadening Your Options

We don't walk alone in this world, and try as we might, we can never entirely escape what we have been and where we have come from. Time and again—and often against my own instincts—the transition coaches I worked with helped me see that the material I was seeking to uncover and structure into a new life was already there. It wasn't a matter of plotting a new architecture; I needed to recognize the infrastructure that already existed and build on that.

One coach exposed me almost literally to the whole universe of possible jobs. Any one of them could be mine. Which did I want? A few months earlier, I think I would have been paralyzed by the experience. Like a kid let loose in a candy store, I wouldn't have known which way to turn. So many goodies, so little time! Now, though, I knew myself better. I was beginning to understand what fit with who I fundamentally was and could be, and what didn't. And indeed, my top five choices from among this universe of infinite possibility were a near-perfect representation of where I had been, where I was, and where I felt I was heading: writer, CEO, publisher, minister, and college president. Clearly, I wanted to integrate ideas and leadership and shape thought. As I looked at the list, I realized that many of the models that had been floating through my head in the preceding months had been half lives, part of the whole person I truly hoped to become. The infrastructure was waiting for me. Now I was getting the blueprint to build that whole person upon it.

Just as important, my coaches also helped me see the barriers I had unconsciously built between myself and fulfillment. On an analysis of motivation, I scored highest on career success, self-actualization, and doing what feels good—a wildly contradictory trio that seemed somehow to fit with my own wild ride through the work world. At the same time, I scored in the bottom decile on tough-mindedness, despite the public image that has been projected onto me for so much of my career. The more I thought about the toll that having to make tough decisions had taken on me, the more I learned about where my best chances for happiness were to be found.

What's truly important in all this is that my possibilities aren't narrowing as I get older; they're broadening. Serial living does that. Each chapter sends out fresh tendrils that we can pick up in later iterations. We draw the strength from where we have been to make something new and creative of where we're going. Jean Hays was an accomplished litigator when it hit her that she never wanted to be in another courtroom in her life. "I want to dance on a table," she told Phil Simhauser of the Center for Executive Options. Phil, in turn, helped her connect her love of the arts with her true talent for getting things done. Today, Jean runs a foundation that supports inner-city kids who want to pursue careers in dance and theater. In hindsight, such chapter shifts seem almost fated, but they're arrived at mostly by hard work.

Of all the drills and exercises I went through with my coaches, none was more effective and valuable than the process that David Zelman calls "generous listening." David, who provides individual coaching through his Transitions Institute (transitionsinstitute.com), insists that you get inside your head and monitor the vital conversations that are going on, but he doesn't stop there. Once you hear the words, you need to take them apart and go deeper and deeper into where they lead you. Working with David, I came to realize how my disappointment with myself grew in the wake of my final months with iVillage. I'd been there when the stock price collapsed. I felt terrible for our investors and our employees. But the more I listened to myself with David's help, the more I realized the need for self-generosity, too. I had made a lot of very good decisions over the whole iVillage span of five and a half years, earning us an enviable category, leadership with a strong brand, and enough cash to survive the "Web winter" of 2000–2001. Yes, the stock had gone into a tailspin under my watch, but so had our whole industry sector. During the falling stage, I had been entirely disoriented. Now, with David's guidance, I'd found clarity. I could let go of defending myself. The sense of freedom was palpable.

There had been a particularly horrible image the very week I'd stepped down as CEO. I'd walked into a party only to find a former colleague I had thought of as one of my close friends and team members at the company schmoozing with the new CEO as though I had never existed. At another table was the boyfriend I'd broken up with that week, with a beautiful blond at his side. Not since junior high had I confronted quite so horrific a sight, all at one time. Life seemed to be going on as though I had never existed.

As David walked me through the moment, though—as he urged me toward self-generosity—I began to see that I hadn't been nearly so slighted as I thought I had been. Why shouldn't an ex-boyfriend have a date? Why shouldn't an important team member schmooze with the new CEO? I even felt that the new CEO was the right one for the company at that moment. The story line had changed, and I deeply desired to grow in different directions. The more generosity I found for myself, the more I uncovered for others. That, too, was a letting go, a relief.

To double-check the entire process and make sure self-delusion hasn't tainted the results, David has his clients deliver a six-question survey to at least five people who know them well: What do you see as my key strengths? What is most distinguishing or unique about me? What, if anything, is bothersome to you about me? What do you, or others, rely on me for—i.e., when the chips are down? Could you tell me something about myself that I don't already know? And if you could wish one thing for me in the next year, what would it be?

In truth, the answers generally resonated with my sense of myself. I was particularly moved by the formidable and unique strengths my reviewers found in me. On the "bothersome" question—a kind of truth gauge for the entire survey—a consistent pattern emerged: I was too quick and pointed in my criticisms. I knew this, but seeing it in black and white gave me a road map. I have supreme control over the precision of the message, David helped me see, but I have to account more for the individual listener and adjust accordingly. Fine, that's doable.

More than anything else, the clarity that I was gaining into and about myself was invaluable. I was preparing to set a new trajectory for my life, and I wanted to travel as lightly as I could into that creation. A year earlier I had told one of my mentees at iVillage that the reason he was stuck was that his ego was leading him around. He fought the message at the moment, but the next day he came to me and said, "Yes, it is," and a week later he was unstuck and on his way to greatness. Now, I had learned something equally useful about myself. One thing that conducting high-level searches teaches you: Even at the top, no one is without liabilities. The person who doesn't know his own liabilities is the one to avoid.

It all counts, the good along with the not so good, and at the end, as a reward for your hard work, you'll have a core of permanent information that can guide you in all successive transitions and career choices. In a world changing as rapidly as the one we live in, this will be the constant, the core attributes you can count on, the ones that will help you find where you can excel and avoid situations where you can't. How can you even begin to put a price tag on that?

The past is not a fixed item. It's raw material waiting to be interpreted anew at each stage of your life. You need to make it talk in these interim periods, and as always, you need to listen to what it says. Carole Hyatt suggests waiting until you get about six months out from the old you and then taking the time to look back again and reanalyze that person.

For the moment, it is all about you. You're building a life from the inside out, and you'll never have a better chance to customize it completely. Take advantage of the opportunity.

One effective way I've found to do that is simply to visit old haunts and tribal grounds as a new person. The gay person who brings his significant other to the reunion of a high school class where he was always thought of as straight, the divorced woman who walks solo into the social function where she was always considered part of a pair, the parents who find themselves sharing beers in a neighborhood bar with old PTA friends after the death of a child are all really testing out new understandings of themselves against the places their past lives were lived out.

In early 2000 I had gone to the Davos World Economic Forum to represent iVillage. Focused intently, almost solely on that goal—as I was always focused intently on the company—I attended virtually every event and panel that seemed to serve iVillage's end. In truth, I didn't learn much that was new or even have that great a time. This year, as my iVillage cycle was winding down, I went back to Davos, but I partook of it completely differently. Leafing through the schedule, I found myself drawn to events with little connection to my titular current life: a session featuring research on language and the brain, a dinner with five of the world's great religious leaders, a very popular dinner on gender and risk, a lunch on the role of algorithms in business—all fascinating and all events I would have talked myself out of attending a year earlier.

As I came to see myself differently during that week in the Swiss Alps, I became, I think, almost literally a different person. One day I ran into Rosabeth Moss Kanter, one of my long-time favorite writers and consultants. An academic attached to the Harvard Business School, Rosabeth has a reputation that extends well beyond Cambridge. By the end of our discussion, we were thinking about my spending a few years at the business school, teaching the things that were now on my mind. The next day, a new dean at Harvard's John F. Kennedy School of Government asked if I would like to come up and teach on social venturing—the great experiments scattered all over the world in using new technologies to combat endemic social problems. After five years of being identified with and identifying myself with an Internet start-up, I was suddenly facing an incredibly exciting world of fresh possibilities, ones that matched my newfound desire to teach, write, mentor, reflect, and influence events through voice instead of the exercise of direct authority. Why, I kept asking myself, had all this happened?

Because I was presenting a new person to the world and the world was reacting to her.

The conversations I had seemed more intense and real in this neutral space of my life than I think they ever could have been in that hyperzone of activity where you have, almost by definition, no time; where you are obsessed with moving an agenda forward; and where you always wear the label of your role. I had no agenda. I had no label to wear. I had time, precious time all to myself, and I could be just what I wanted to be. Near the end of the gathering, I posed in a leopard-skin dress with two of my buddies for a famous Italian fashion photographer—a shot that later appeared, full page, in *Talk* magazine. As I was leaving Davos, I remember thinking that if I were still in my CEO costume, I would never have been able to do something so spontaneous, but that's the blessing of this walk in the desert: There's space; there's a broadness of focus that will narrow to a laser-like intensity once you've found the absolute expression of the next you. Treasure it. Trust it. Use it.

> Be prepared to be stunned. As you present a new person to the world, completely new opportunities come your way.

Finding the Words

Of all the transition programs I've worked through and studied, David Zelman's is the least likely to be mass-produced. At $30,000 for four days, David is at the high end of the business—he works mostly with venture capitalists and bankers—but he occupies the high end in wisdom and effectiveness, too. And he's certainly the extreme in terms of the demands he puts on you and the emotional and physical expenditure he expects you to make. Making a transition with David must be much like training for the Green Berets: not for wimps or the half-committed, but a great ride all the same and worth every second of the pain when you head back into battle.

For David, the absolute core of the experience is reinventing the conversation inside your own head, because it is there—in the midst of those words—that you find the direction that drives all action. To get you there, he breaks the learning process into five stages: taking responsibility for your past, accepting your life to date, assessing who you are and what is possible, exploring pathways to the future, and developing the personal infrastructure to keep you on the selected path (see Mapping Your Core Work Profile on page 95). For David, the sense of falling that is so common to transitions is explained by the fact that most people are so deeply rooted in their own pasts that they can't find the words for new creation. Without the necessary vocabulary, it's impossible to become the author of your own experience, and without claiming authorship of your life, there's no way to go forward with it. You're suspended forever in that space between then and next.

"I train people in what I call 'the language of the future,'" he told me. "Most people are stuck in the language of the past. Who you are today, how you experience yourself and others intrinsically is a product of the past primarily because of your relationship with language. If you can shift and recognize what the language of the future is, then you begin to relocate yourself there."

Core Values	Mission Statement	Life Aspirations (12 Goals Governing Creation)	Myers-Briggs Type	Areas of Prior Peak Performance	Lifestyle Preferences
1. Family centered 2. Spiritually rich 3. High commitment 4. Humor/Fun 5. Aesthetically pleasing 6.	I care deeply about my family, creating a home life that gathers family and friends in a warm, communal cocoon, providing a sense of family and continuity. I give my children a foundation of values, self-respect, self-discipline, and encourage them to pursue interests and acquire skills so that life always seems inventive to them. I am a friend who helps my friends live their best lives, who encourages them. I am a person who has created influential brands which help millions around the world to live the best lives possible. I have had the courage of my convictions to prevail over doubts and occasional unpopularity and teach other people to be able to keep the cause under all conditions.	1. Family centered home life 2. Creation of culture-shaping business 3. 4. 5. 6. 7. 8. 9. 10. 11. 12.	INFJ	1. From chairman 2. Trials of life 3. Creating company 4.	1. Schedule 2. Level of responsibility 3. Environment 4. Geography 5. Stress level 6. Risk 7. Degree of freedom

Areas of Past Failures (Situations to Avoid)	What Others Can Count on You For	Ideal Job Fits	Ideal Functionality Fits	Key Strengths	Ranking Next Chapter
1. Slow growth situations 2. Excessive political env 3. Formal, stiff environments 4. 5. 6. 7.	1. Perseverance 2. Will to win 3. Direct perceptive feedback 4. 5. 6. 7.	1. College president 2. Publisher 3. 4. 5. 6. 7.	1. Leading in challenging situations 2. Leading small, high-performance teams 3. Writing/communicating 4. Visioning 5. 6. 7. 8. 9. 10. 11.	1. Strategist 2. Inspiring teams 3. Visionary 4. Brand builder 5. 6. 7.	Spirituality Money Status Place you are coming from 1. Inspiration 2. Wisdom 3. Courage

Mapping Your Core Work Profile

To help you find those words, to guide you across the chasm, to help you begin to leave yesterday and today and start into tomorrow, David insists that his clients get very real about their own experiences, very quickly: That's the drill sergeant at work. Only by accurately identifying the past can you make the focus shifts that will reorient you in the present and put solid ground beneath your feet, and David doesn't mean for you to fail at the task.

Maybe you had a boss you resented or one you feel you failed in some way. Perhaps you feel you should have left your job sooner or left it better. Maybe it's your subordinates who are holding you back in the past—you failed to lead them, they failed to follow you—or a former wife, or lover, or guilt over children you didn't attend to properly. Whatever it is, and "it" can be almost anything, David doesn't let go until you have finished with it once and for all, and the matter or the person or the incident won't take another calorie of your energy.

I know, all this can sound very touchy-feely, but not until you've been through the process and can feel the physical sense of release that comes from letting go, do you realize just how much of our present tense can be occupied by these regrets and unsolved dilemmas from the past. I had come to intellectual terms with the end of my long work and personal relationship with Nancy Evans. I'd even understood what had happened to us. But not until David led me through an extraordinarily painful moment-by-moment examination of Nancy's and my time together and the degree to which we had both put the business first could I really let go of the emotional baggage I had been hauling around with me.

In David's words, "If you own what happened, then you can move on more quickly." By contrast, if you don't claim ownership, you'll always be leading a life that has been scripted in part by some other author.

Money

Ultimately, what you're trying to get out of this walk in the desert is the compass that will keep you headed in the right direction. The next job isn't there quite yet—we'll come to that soon enough—but the map to get you to the next job is starting to make sense. If you're lucky like Barry Diller, you've been able to make this journey unimpeded by the practical constraints of putting a roof over your head or food on the table. If not, you can at least be more creative about what you do to meet your basic needs, for the simple reason that you should know so much more about yourself and where you are headed. You're not fleeing the past anymore; you're pursuing the future. That can make the sacrifices easier, and there are other resources to draw on.

Chris Ogden had almost no reserves lined up when he left his career as a TV packager to become a therapist. What he had saved over the years had gone to support his family and fund a divorce. But Chris had an attitude that said this is what I have to do and this is what will have to happen, and that attitude gave him the confidence to make his dream come true. Within three months of making the decision to change his life, Chris had earned as much as he had in the previous two years, enough to meet the entire cost of his new professional training.

Writing this book has been for me a sort of working girl's equivalent of Barry Diller's trek across America, a way to pay the bills while pursuing the questions most on my mind. Donald Marrs may have hit upon the best solution I've ever run across. Having risen to the prestigious rank of vice president and creative director with Leo Burnett in Chicago, Don talked his boss and mentor into, in effect, demoting him to a role producing commercials at the ad agency's L.A. outpost, where he could begin to try on his new skin as a filmmaker. "Although exhausted, I felt I had pulled off a great coup," he writes. "I had stolen my life back and now had the corporation working for me." To do that, though, Don Marrs had to first know who "me" now was, which gets to the larger point to be made here: Whatever you do to meet the bills, if anything, you should be leaving this desert journey with a knowledge of your core attributes, of the infrastructure you need to build upon: invaluable information. If you don't understand yourself better than you did at the start of this trek—the self you were and the self you are and the self you are in the process of becoming—then you're not ready to end it.

The Unique You

"Most people describe themselves by trace qualities," David Zelman told me when we were going through his boot camp. "I'm more interested in who people are at the human level. If I can get you back to being that, as opposed to being 48 years old and chairman of iVillage and whatever other qualities you might ascribe to yourself, then you're getting back to being a human being and you can begin to start to tap into what your gifts are.

"What is it that's unique about you on this planet? What is it that people count on you for? All this stuff starts to mean something. Inside your own experience is this new awareness of who you are for yourself and for others. You start going in a different direction. Different things open up. You become available to a different universe that's already there but that you didn't have access to before. In a sense, that's what I do: I give people access to themselves."

From the outside, jobs have a cookie-cutter look: A sales manager is a sales manager is a sales manager. Inside, of course, no two jobs or companies are the same. But until you gain access to yourself, until you know what cluster of interests and motivations is most likely to bring you the greatest level of happiness, you will always be stumbling in the dark. Work doesn't have to feel like work. Make the right match, fit the unique you to a situation uniquely for you, and work begins to feel like play.

After going through an ugly firing hatched in boardroom politics, my brother developed his own interest cluster and condensed it into a mission statement. Henceforth, he declared, he would "work only with people I like and respect and . . . only where I feel I can make a difference." It sounds simple almost, but when you practice those principles rigorously as my brother has done, it can change the direction of everything.

My own mission statement is still forming as I write. It needs more definition, more editing. But when I made a point of writing it down the other day, it came out like this: "To do things that can be done from a feminine persona (I'm handing in my warrior studs), to influence the ability of successful individuals, who in turn influence all of the people who work for them, to face this new century with the internal fluidity they will need to make and use change to their advantage. And I want to share my wisdom and capacity to create, not shoot at anyone in a competitive battle."

It's a mouthful, to be sure, but David Zelman has helped me see that it signals a huge shift. In my old life I had been aspiring to fearlessness, brilliance, and independence. In this new life, I find myself more drawn toward wisdom, courage, and inspiration. What gets me out of bed in the morning has changed. Learning what those new things are unleashes a powerful force as we prepare to go out into the world. In David's words, it gives us access to ourselves.

CHAPTER FIVE

Stirrings

*The beginnings . . . of all human undertakings
are untidy.*

—John Galsworthy

Gaining access to yourself, in David Zelman's memorable phrase, will give you a clearer sense of who you are and what you want. It will tell you what constraints you have to deal with in pursuing your future, from family and children to the constraints imposed by your own uniqueness. Most important, perhaps, gaining access will give you a window into what you are truly great at. Now you need to get very good at something else that can be just as hard: listening to this self that you have worked so hard to gain entry to—not just to the surface sounds but to the deep inner voices, too.

What are the possibilities that have been pulling on you that you have yet to acknowledge, even to your conscious self? What are the conversations that you can't seem to get out of your mind? Some of them will have been self-contained—the private "what ifs?" and "could I's?" that pepper our interior monologues. Others may be the result of a chance encounter at a dinner party or with a cabin mate at 35,000 feet—a snippet of talk that suggested a road not taken that ever since has been resonating deep within, like some central personal tuning fork. These are more than aural residue. They stick with us for a reason: because they are the beginning of our dialogue with our own destiny.

Loren Stell was trained as a minister but spent 19 years as a journalist with little hope of breaking into the big time. For one thing, he's dyslexic. More critical, his work wasn't married to his passion. As the years went along, though, he developed a keen interest in fairy tales that blossomed finally into an obsession, and as that happened, he began to reconnect to his past at the same time that he started scripting his future. In time, Loren used his religious training to help him get to the deeper meanings of the tales that so intrigued him. That led him to interpretation and to the interplay between stories, symbols, and dreams. Today, Loren is a successful therapist who urges his clients to put their dreams into poetry.

Things connect if we let them. The first thing my friend Ally did when a divorce left her with little money and a daughter in grade school was to sign on with a local catering firm. Ally was famous among her friends for her bold and imaginative cooking. At the catering firm, though, she was living inside someone else's food dreams, and doing so under a ton of institutional restraints. After two years of slaving, she built up enough of a cash reserve to take a month off and plan her own business, one that would allow her to pursue her other great interest: early American textiles. Over the next decade, that effort would balloon into a successful wholesale business that used subcontractors as far away as India and Thailand. Ally sold her interest in the company as her daughter was finishing college, remarried, and began looking after her own aging parents and her new husband's mother, who was by then nearing the century mark. Today, Ally is a major domo with an assisted-living center only a few minutes' drive from her house.

Whenever I get together with Ally, I'm reminded of how successfully she has adjusted her work chapters to the rhythms of her life — the good moments and the trying ones. The catering business was the wrong road for her, but so often, I've found, these first intimations are likely to be flawed. What's important isn't the misdirection, but the fact that she worked through it and came out on the other side of her rein-vention to true joy. I see her ex-husband occasionally, too, at parties that pull our old circle of friends together. He remar-ried shortly after their divorce and left his corporate job as a compensation specialist to open a consulting business where he did just the same thing. He has done well — outsourcing became the name of the game just as he outsourced him-self — but the repetition of the same small skill set has taken its toll over the years. There's a dullness to him; he has aged faster than he should have.

Futures are built by listening to ourselves and by taking our stirrings seriously. Our lives are awash with intimations of where we are headed. The people we envy, the jobs we covet, the lifestyles we want to lead, the rewards we dream might be ours — they're all messages in a bottle, silent telegrams self-addressed that fill us with stirrings, visions of other realities that we might walk into, if only we will open and read them. Too often, though, we don't. Too often, we stuff the message back in the bottle. We turn and walk, and sometimes run, the other way. We blind ourselves intentionally or unintentionally to these premonitions of reinvention because they scare us. They portend disruption. They suggest discontents with our present realities that we are not willing to deal with in our waking, conscious lives. Instead of nurturing our stirrings, we root them out before they can begin to take hold and grow.

As I began to drift loose from my entrepreneurial chapter, I was terrified that some of my stirrings would disrupt my comfortable New York lifestyle. I told Chris Ogden that I would be happy to look deeply into them as soon as Nasdaq returned my paper wealth to a more comfortable level. Until then, I would just put them on ice. Because he's far more courageous than I—and also not hooked on Versace—Chris would have none of it. "What a cop-out!" he told me. "Don't you trust the universe at all?"

"Birth is a hideous thing," Barry Diller once told me, with his usual fierce iconoclasm. As anyone who has ever attended one will attest, Barry couldn't be more right. Husbands who have been through war faint at the sight of their offspring coming into the world. There's blood. There's goop. There's this howling little thing. But without birth there is no life, and without allowing ourselves to be reborn, there is no reinvention either.

> Beginnings are messy and indistinct, but don't let the absence of a clear demarcation discourage or fool you. These are moments of great power to create your world.

Like real birth, this is a process without guarantees. To pursue our stirrings is to risk failure, even heartbreak, and the more strongly these possibilities pull on us, the worse any failure and heartbreak will be. True tragedy, as the Greeks knew, requires falling from a great height, even if it's only a great height we have allowed ourselves to believe in. An infinitesimal fraction of those who dream of winning a Nobel Prize will ever be flown to Stockholm to receive the award. Only a tiny some of us who aspire to write a commercially successful novel will ever get to see our names on a best-seller list. If everyone could get to the top, it wouldn't be a top. Even when we win our dream, there's no assurance that the rewards will be what we expected. Money doesn't buy happiness; winning time to stay at home with our children doesn't come with a warranty on domestic bliss. But it's also a safe bet that everyone who ever received a Nobel Prize or wrote a best-selling novel or built a great company from the ground up listened at some point in his life to the stirrings toward greatness and importance and magnitude, if not in himself then in the work he undertook, in whatever field it was honored in.

That's the point: Our dreams may not tell us where we'll end up, but they do point to the path we need to set out on. And here's the larger issue: We live today in a world in which we can take those paths time and time again if we really listen and really hear and know who we are to begin with and who we are becoming.

Burning Bushes

As I told friends and colleagues about this book, and as I spoke about its themes at formal and informal gatherings, the most frequent request I got was this: "Please focus on how to really know what you want to do next. . . . That's where I get so confused."

The real answer is the one I just gave: We all have deep within us the stirrings that are waiting to tell us the path to set out on. Success is getting what *you* specifically want, as David Zelman points out. For a kid, that might be a new bike. For an adult, the world of choices is infinite. The harder answer, though, is that there is no telling when this real answer will arrive, no timetable for when these stirrings will rise to the surface and begin to take shape and form. The more reinvention you open yourself to, the more chapters you live through and exhaust and move out of, the easier all this becomes. That I believe, but even for those of us who have been living this way for decades, there are only patterns to watch for, not givens to expect.

Some futures arrive with what seems like startling suddenness. Like Paul on the road to Damascus, we round a bend, and out of the blue, we're struck blind by new purpose and intent. But like Paul—who, as the pharisee Saul, had left for Damascus "breathing out threatenings and slaughter against the disciples of the Lord"—we're also likely to have been building to these moments for years upon years.

I don't know of anyone who ever had a more clear and powerful realization of purpose than Craig Cohon. One moment he was a Coca-Cola executive; virtually the next, he had decided to give it all up to begin the Global Legacy foundation. In the movies, it would be one of those scenes where a person walks in a door as one man and walks out the other side of the door as someone else. In the Bible, a bush would burst into flames. In the real world we live in, it would take nearly half a year for Craig to put his plan into effect, but it was his whole life that had prepared him for the epiphany triggered by Bill Clinton's speech at Davos.

Working for Coke for three and a half years in Russia, Craig had seen head-on the social dislocation caused by the triumph of democratic capitalism. In Tibet on his honeymoon, he had been so appalled by the poverty he encountered that he asked Coke to provide a series of coaches to help align his social and corporate consciences. Out of that experience had come a mission statement that, in hindsight, pointed him precisely toward where he was headed. Craig determined that he wanted "to bring together powerful and effective leaders to bring about collective action." At Global Legacy, he has been enrolling CEOs of major corporations to take collective responsibility for ending the most pressing problems on the planet, and doing so in their own lifetimes: the same mission he had been on at Coke, only differently interpreted and applied to social, not corporate, ends. Craig's epiphany was, in fact, more like an earthquake caused by deep fractures that had long been building toward the surface, just as his resolution of it was the rounding off of multiple decades of concern and experience.

"My core purpose," Craig says, "is bringing together a diverse group of visionary leaders to make something magical happen. I did it in high school. I did it in university. I did it in Russia with Coke. I'm doing it now, and you know what? It's connecting me to Russia. It's connecting me to what I did in university. It's a connection, all a connection."

The exercises my transition coaches put me through didn't turn up anything completely new: I've had powerful stirrings for years now toward the ministry. I know that someday I'll attend divinity school. But I also know this is not the time to realize that chapter of my life. I have my little girls. I have aspirations for them that involve an income no one can or should expect to pull down in the ministry. I'm also not entirely divorced from my own list of material wants that seem, at least on the surface, antithetical to this cloth that attracts me. And I'm still interested in start-ups and in venture capital, the money and counsel that fuel them.

Still, I nurture that chapter along with other chapters-to-be because I truly believe that, given good health, I will get to live them all. I nurture the stirrings that inform them, too, and the longer I do that and the more everything incubates, the more—like Craig Cohon—things just seem to come together. Not long ago, I came upon not one but two ordained ministers who are partners in very successful venture firms. Both had attended divinity school while working as venture capitalists. At Yale Divinity School, I found four CEOs in residence, studying for theology degrees. I wasn't even surprised by these encounters because by now I have a model for how the threads of a life come together and can be customized.

Bill Strickland was well into his thirties when he began his remarkable Manchester Craftsmen Skills program as a way of using art to help kids in the same impoverished Pittsburgh neighborhood where he had grown up, but the stirring that impelled him had been building for two decades, born in a high school art course that had served as both a refuge and inspiration for Strickland and many others like him.

"My art teacher, Mr. Ross, created a warm, intimate environment. It was very safe, very predictable. It got me away from the high school population to a place that I could rely on. He brought in music. He had a coffeepot. There was lots of clay. He brought in books on architecture and crafts, and I just got immersed in this whole world of human possibility.

"I actually think I had what I would call a religious experience. I'm not a big church guy—I'm kind of on the other side. But one weekend when I was 16 years old, I saw Mr. Ross make this ceramic dresser in the art room, and I had a vision of how life could be. I saw him, and he was in light, bathed in what I call the light of Saturday afternoon. I saw it, and I said, 'I've got to do that. I'm going there. I'm going toward that light because it will take me out of the darkness.' And the darkness was my neighborhood and my life experience and all that, and the light was the arts. That was the portal that had opened up, and I was absolutely right.

"The possibilities are endless if you have the right imagination and if you have the right set of values, and if exploration and excitement and mystery are something you draw energy from."

Even then, Bill Strickland might never have gotten his center off the ground if he hadn't been so uncompromisingly true to the stirrings that he carried forward from his high school years. When push came to shove and the fate of the center hung in the balance, Bill got some terrific advice and settled for more rather than less.

"I was in a real bad place with my center," Bill told me. "I wasn't getting enough money to run it. I'd heard about a guy named Father Cunningham—Bill Cunningham, a Catholic priest in Detroit who had built an organization called Focus Hope. So I went and saw him and told him about my problems, and he said, 'You're smart enough to out-fox these people. What I would encourage you to do is expand your vision, not limit it.' I said, 'Well, that's against all conventional wisdom,' and he said, 'Yes, but that's how you got where you are now.'

"So I made it bigger. Now it's a whole seven-acre community that includes housing and the arts, and I was able to do it because he provided that portal. He opened it up and said, 'The answer is right there in front of your face.' He gave me the confidence to walk through that and say, 'Okay, I got the smarts, I got the encouragement from this guy. He's done it. I can do it.' Now I want to build a community that will be bigger and better than the one he built.

"I'd become frozen and stuck. I didn't know what to do. My energy had become weird; I was inefficient about using my talent. But by his helping me to revive and improve and even enlarge my vision, I was able to get back into motion and to convert that movement to fuel. It becomes self-perpetuating: Vision provides the fuel, and the fuel provides vision, and you're back in the game. My therapist had told me the same thing: 'Build the best training center in the United States of America,' he said, 'because for you, if you don't do that, it won't be worth anything.'"

Bill's therapist was right, in more ways than one. The more uncompromising your vision, the less chance you will cheat on yourself. And the less you cheat on yourself, the more fully you will find yourself in the Zone, where every sacrifice you've made will find its reward.

Les Guffman had been a producer and writer for *NBC News* in the early and mid-1980s, and then in the late 1980s had signed on as senior producer for *USA Today*, the TV show based on the newspaper. When this show failed after an expensive year in development and a relatively short time on air, Les decided to strike out on his own.

"I just told myself that I was going to produce my own programs from now on. I had worked for too many mediocre executive producers. I wasn't going to work for anyone else. I started with the Robert Kennedy Human Rights Award. It had been given for 10 years in a public ceremony at Georgetown University. I'd been to one of them—it was a marvelous event—but the ceremony had never been televised."

Les took his idea to WETA, the public TV channel based in Washington, D.C., which agreed to provide the crew and technical support. To make sure he wasn't getting carried away by his own idea, he ran it by Tom Brokaw, whom he had come to know at *NBC News*. Brokaw not only loved the idea, but agreed to host the ceremony.

"This was 1989—Tiananmen Square, the fall of the Berlin Wall. The award was being presented to Fang Lizi, the Chinese dissident and astrophysicist. He had taken refuge in the U.S. Embassy in Beijing and was still there, but there were other dissidents in the audience who had managed to get away. We were set to go on national TV by tape delay that evening at nine o'clock, prime time on PBS. That morning, Tom flies in from Berlin, where he's been covering the fall of the Wall live. Tom is introducing Lech Walesa, who's to give the keynote speech, when he pulls a piece of the Berlin Wall out of his pocket and hands it to Lech. It just sent chills down everyone's spine. Tom was wonderful. It was the first thing I ever produced on my own, and it was a magnificent program."

Les would go on to bring *Discover Magazine* to TV—it was his idea that became the signature program of the Discovery Channel. As I write, he's the head of TV for *Outside* magazine, but it all goes back, he says, to his decision to produce his own TV programs more than a decade earlier and to his determination not to cheat on himself or his vision when he did it. As with Bill Strickland, the purity of the desire became its own reward.

A final word on this subject of epiphanies: Not every one may be right for us, but exploring each of them that seems right can lead us to the deeper strata where the real foundation and stirrings often lie. A friend who has spent his professional lifetime on the faculty of some of America's most prestigious private secondary schools—schools that claim senators and captains of industry among their alumni—told me that for years he had harbored a vision of himself as a headmaster of a school very much like the ones he has taught at.

"By the time I was 40, I'd worked my way from chairman of the history department to dean of students and assistant head for the upper school, and then I just sat and waited. Almost every time a vacancy came up somewhere, I'd get a call. All the headhunters knew about me; I met with search committees all over the place. But I never got the last call. I don't know what it was—I was public school myself, and that always seemed to come up somehow. You know: 'of them, but not them.' My wife had gone to a good private school and she taught science part time. Our kids were respectable. Even with the slight glitch of my high school degree, I thought we were a dream team. Apparently not.

"I'd just turned 45 when a woman I met at a party told me about what she called the 'Obituary Test.' 'It's how I decide how serious a goal is for me,' she said. 'I imagine that whatever it is doesn't appear in my obituary. Then I lie in my grave and try to think about how much regret I would have over its absence.'

"So I did that. I came back to the school a week later, two weeks before fall term, by myself. My wife had taken the kids to visit her parents. I spent a whole day—10 hours, from breakfast to dinner—doing just what the woman had suggested. I even typed out my name in boldface and then underneath, in small type, I put 'Headmaster,' the way an obituary might look in the *New York Times*. And I just sat there and looked at it, and tried to think about how it made me feel. About six o'clock, just for the hell of it, I deleted 'Headmaster' and put 'Teacher' in its place. It was cheating, in a way—the *Times* would never give an obit to a plain teacher—but the effect was absolutely riveting.

"'Headmaster' was only going to tell the world that I'd been good at raising money, good at handling litigious parents and holding widows' hands, good at keeping the school's name out of the papers in all the worst ways. I've served under three headmasters, and I only liked two of those and respected just one. Even though it would never make the *Times*, 'Teacher' would say that I had done something with my life that I could really feel good about. I'd imparted knowledge. Maybe I'd made a difference in lives that had made a difference in other lives.

"Two days later, I went into the Headmaster's office and told him that I intended to step down at the end of the new term as Head of Upper School. I wanted to teach, and if I couldn't do it there, I'd do it somewhere else. I had to fight to get my classes back—the people who were teaching them seemed to know what I had just learned—but I did. I got my classes back, and I've never been happier."

As with Loren Stell during his years as a journalist, my teacher friend had trapped himself in a no-win position. Maybe he would have made a great headmaster. Maybe he even should have been a headmaster: Something had clearly been calling him in that direction. But by the time he finally confronted the ambition, his stirrings had moved on to somewhere else, and his ambition was part of someone else's story line.

What's the common thread between all these stories? Simply this, I think: that by hook or by crook, every one of these people opened themselves up to their specific yearnings, and by doing so, they began to create their realities.

Convergence happens. All the threads of your past ultimately will be woven together as you become an accomplished creator.

The Art of the Possible

When my friend Karen Quinn was laid off from American Express after 17 years, we got together to explore her options. What were her stirrings, I asked her? What were the inner voices saying? The question seemed to throw her off guard, but after a while, Karen answered that she wished she could paint for a living. She'd been doing so as an amateur since she was a girl—wonderful canvasses that fill her home. If she could do anything she wanted, she said, she'd paint full time now. But, she added quickly, that would be impossible. There were the bills, the financial obligations she and her husband had undertaken. Besides, painting was a million miles from her career in marketing.

The response was typical. Karen had received a severance package from American Express. She had the means to take five or six months for her own reinvention. But we're all threatened to a greater or lesser degree by change of the magnitude that following her dream would have imposed. Keep the dream alive, I advised her. That's all. You don't have to act on it, but let it sit there on the side as you plan for what lies ahead. Four months later, Karen was on her way to creating a business that she projects will bring in a sufficient level of income to allow her to take a day off a week. That way, she can also pursue her painting career to see if she can make it as a professional artist.

"We forget how indirect and unimpressive beginnings really are," Bill Bridges writes, "and we imagine instead some clear and conscious steps we ought to be taking. Think back to the important beginnings in your own past. You bumped into an old friend that you hadn't seen for years, and he told you about a job at his company that opened up just that morning. You met your spouse-to-be at a party that you really hadn't wanted to go to and that you almost skipped. You learned to play the guitar while you were getting over the measles, and you learned French because the Spanish class met at 8:00 a.m. and you hated to get up that early. . . . The lesson in all such experiences is that when we are ready to make a beginning, we will shortly find an opportunity."

That, I think, is really what happened to Karen Quinn. She was ready to make a beginning, and she found an opportunity to include her stirrings toward art in that beginning. Or maybe more accurately, the opportunity found her because when we open ourselves to possibility, when we put our searching, restless selves out in the world, when we truly try to align our dreams with our realities and let serendipity wash over us, amazing things can take place.

For Matthew Hoffman, the kind of stirrings that moved Karen Quinn came in the side door, in the form of a bad back—not once, but twice. Hoffman was in his late twenties, working in construction in New Mexico, where he had grown up, when back pain forced him into a state program for the disabled.

"This was a program for people at loss, people at risk of being on social welfare for the rest of their lives," Matthew told me. "I went to the University of New Mexico on the state's dime and realized I knew how to write, which came out of the blue. By my senior year, I was working as a stringer for the *Albuquerque Journal*."

Matthew's journalistic career would eventually land him a job as a health writer and later a book editor at Rodale Press, the protean magazine and book publisher in Emmaus, Pennsylvania, an hour's commute north of Philadelphia, where he and his wife, Chris, were living.

"After nine years at Rodale, I was tired, discouraged with the whole corporate structure, but I tend to stick with whatever I'm doing because the idea of change terrifies me. Chris and I had been talking for a year about my trying a freelance career, but I was afraid to leave the paycheck, and I guess I didn't believe it was possible to do it—to make any kind of living as a freelancer. I'd probably still be at Rodale if my back hadn't gone out again. With the herniated disk, I couldn't do the commute anymore. I couldn't sit at a desk for eight hours. It forced me to make a change I wanted to do anyway—it forced me onto the honest track. Chris and I had decided that if I was able to make two-thirds of my Rodale salary, we'd be good. If I made half, we'd be okay. In the first year, I more than doubled what I'd been making."

Even then, Matthew says, he was not out of the woods. The long hours he'd worked at Rodale stretched into even longer hours as a freelancer, until he found himself averaging

60 hours a week. Moving back to Albuquerque has helped some, he says, but it wasn't until he consciously started to cut his workweek in half, aiming at 30 hours, that he began to find a balance between his job and the rest of his life.

"I still define myself an awful lot by my work," he told me, "so I'm not really comfortable with this, but I'm starting to realize that it's okay to soak up some sun during the day or take a nap in the afternoon. It's not wasted time; it's quality time. I'd had a lot of pressure from Chris—'We have to get to some sort of life that doesn't involve careers,' she kept saying. But I've been freelancing for three years now, and I'm just starting to come into touch with the idea of what it is I want to do, how to live a life that feels like it's mine."

I often think of this period of free-floating exploration in terms of the old children's game "hot and cold." Some paths are false leads, some true ones, but you'll never find out which are which until you get out in the world, until you put yourself in play and begin following all the tiny instincts and clues that have been building in you. Believe me, the "hots" and "colds" are waiting—you have an internal beeper system that's ready to go. At this point, you just have to give it a chance to work. Besides, after all the hard work you've been doing, this time actually can be fun. You're meeting people. You're casting a wide net. All you're searching for is the match that your internal compass is leading you toward. Making the match succeed is over the next hill, just out of sight. What's not to like?

Three times in my career I've set out on similar searches, and all three times opportunity found me at the same time I found it. I knew a full year before I left American Express that it had become a "no-place" for me. I wanted to be in the media business, and Amex wasn't. I wanted to be in an environment where fun was a stronger part of the ethic and where individual eccentricity counted for more. Neither of those was American Express either, for good reasons: Generally, we don't trust our money or credit ratings to wild and crazy places. For personal reasons, I also wanted to move to Washington, D.C. Finally, I told a few people about the stirrings that had been building, including my boss, and within a week, his brother had offered me a job at what was then the Time-Life Video and Film unit, headquartered in Alexandria, Virginia, just across the Potomac from where I wanted to be. Bingo.

Four years later, I felt a notion building in me to start a new-media company with a strong brand presence. I was heading into an entrepreneurial chapter. The people I found myself envying were doing just what I wanted to do; the voices inside me were saying this is where I was headed next. I was consulting for a few clients, including America Online. Six months after the urging that became iVillage had first taken root, AOL offered me the seed money to begin making our dream come true. Had I gone to work for AOL in the expectation of funding? No, not at any conscious level, certainly. But because I had listened to my stirrings, I had put myself in a position to win.

This time around, as I was relishing this "no-place" between jobs, someone asked for my assistance in creating a new company that would use the newest technology to match people to their work. I was glad to help—the subject had become a consuming interest in any event—but as I got into the project, I began to have a mental picture of bringing six or seven similar small companies together to create a leader in the field. I didn't want to commit to actually do anything yet, but it was there, rattling around in my head, when a call came in from a highly regarded angel fund — a group that brings talent, funding, and companies together — asking me to lead its efforts in exactly the same area.

Carl Jung, the legendary psychoanalyst, talks about all this as *synchronicity*. The larger message might be that whatever is in your head, there's likely to be an opportunity out in the world just waiting for you to find it. In this case, I was shaping a future on the fly, but because I had listened to my stirrings, the future was becoming just what I wanted it to be. I'd opened myself to opportunity; and opportunity, as it so often does when we finally get in touch with our desires, came pouring in.

Laws of Probability

Opportunity feeds on itself. I'm convinced of that. But I'm also convinced that the more precisely we define our dreams, the more we can convert possibility to probability. An example that may at first seem trivial but that I hope will prove a bigger point:

As I was making the transition out of iVillage into my new life, I knew that I wanted a personal office — a space outside of my house where I could think, write, and hold creative work sessions. The space, I decided, had to be within a two-block radius of my apartment: I wanted to be near my girls. The feeling I was after in the interior could also come only from a converted brownstone. I wanted history. I wanted charm. Anything that said "corporate" was verboten. Besides, I wanted to be able to use the space as a kind of extension of my own residence: Friends, colleagues, people I was working with on specific projects could stay there if they had to, or if I was lost in some project after my girls were asleep, I could just curl up there at night, surrounded by my books and papers. In practical terms, that meant a full bath and at least a rudimentary kitchen. What's more, I was looking to rent, not buy. I was looking to shed responsibilities, not add to them.

Once I had a clear idea of what the space would look and feel like and where it would be, I called a broker and described it to her: the close proximity to my home, the brownstone, everything. Anyone familiar with New York, a city where the high cost and scarcity of decent domiciles makes real estate the topic of every other conversation, will not be surprised by her response. "You are out of your mind," she told me. "It will be months and could well be years before anything like you have described even comes on the market." Bottom line, she said: You'll have to broaden your parameters. No, I told her, here's the bottom line: I don't have to broaden my parameters, and I won't. This is what I want, and you'll see, it will happen.

Two days later, she called back. I still remember her words: "You must be living right. I found everything you want a block from your home — a whole floor of a landmark brownstone." "That's great," I told her, "but I have one more request." I could hear her draw in her breath as I spoke: "I need to sublet the space for three months before I'm ready to move in." When she stopped laughing, I told her, "Just ask the landlord." The next day she called me back again: "Unbelievable," she began, "I did ask the landlord, and he has a journalist friend from Italy who's coming for three months and looking for a sublet."

Today, as I write, I'm in that space. There's a kitchenette behind me and a fireplace directly across from where I work most days. The damper is bum, the place tends to fill with smoke when I light a fire, but all the same. . . . To my left, a pair of windows look out across 74th Street. To my right is a large back room with a four-poster French country bed and a desk for my assistant and, beyond that, a full bath and the door to a deck that most days is washed in sunshine and bursting with wild roses.

Was it all just sheer real estate luck? Maybe, but I don't think so. If I had given the broker wider parameters, I'm convinced she would still be looking, and I'd still have towering stacks of books and papers littering my dining room table. The precise image of what I needed focused her attention, and once her attention was focused, she could see what was really there. Time and again, I've found it easier to create exactly what I want than to mount a broad search in the hopes of narrowing it eventually to something satisfactory. Seeing patterns instead of clutter is the key: Specificity creates opportunity.

> The more exact your dream, the faster you will get there. It's easier to achieve something very specific than to reach a general goal.

One more way to make the laws of probability work for you: Go and meet the people who excite you the most. Drink their blood, if only for a few minutes. I know this can seem impossible—the more someone inspires envy, the busier she or he is likely to be, and the harder to look in the eye—but my experience has taught me that you can get to almost anyone you want to get to, and you don't have to spend a lifetime networking to do it. A really great letter or e-mail can open the door. Assure the person that you don't want a job, that you're not selling anything, and that you'll need no more than 30 minutes and more likely 15. Once you're in the door, don't succumb to the temptation to hustle. Accomplished, powerful people are hustled all the time. Far more rarely are they asked, with no expectation of immediate gain, how they did it and who they are. That's the best kind of flattery.

> Drink the blood of those you envy. They are your path.

At a Matrix Award dinner not long ago, Cathy Black was telling about a note she received two decades ago, when she was running *Ms.* magazine. Valerie Salembier, who wrote the note, wasn't looking for a job; she just wanted to say how much *Ms.* meant to her. In large part because she wasn't seeking one, Cathy gave Valerie a job and started her on a career path that would eventually land her as VP and publisher of *Esquire*. Now, two decades later, Valerie was receiving the Matrix Award.

I've refined my own list for these drink-the-blood interviews to five basics: What is it like to be you? What was important in creating this position, or company, or life? What were the most important three or four forks in the road and how did you approach them? What don't you like about what you do now? And what do you want to be next? I don't claim any special genius in that list, but I can learn a lot through it in a very short time, including how the person feels about evolution and transition. And I'm always astonished how often a failure to fit in or get along with an important boss was part of the process that pushed the person forward into a next and better chapter. If nothing else, you'll come away from such a session with the sure knowledge that almost no experience can be judged a failure. We humans learn through mistakes and adversity. We learn our way to finding our place in the world. Sometimes we even learn our way to our first $100 million.

Part of what you're doing here is simply visualizing yourself in a role—getting a mental image of the kind of person you are seeking to become. When I left business school, I began calling on the senior vice presidents and CEOs of the companies I was working for. They were whom I wanted to be, and I wanted to know as much as I could learn about who that was and what it entailed. As my entrepreneurial drive strengthened and as I began to realize that I wanted to create a unique new-media brand, I began to hone in on Barry Diller; David Geffen, who started a billion dollar record label; Gerry Laybourne, who created the multibillion dollar brand Nickelodeon; and John Hendricks, who converted his quirky conviction that people would spend their leisure time watching footage of wild animals and learning about the natural world into the Discovery Network.

I was doing more than simply trying on their skin. I was past that stage—I knew what I wanted to become. Now I wanted to know not just how that vision might walk and talk and even think, but also how it accessorized itself, how it fit into its environment, what kind of ecosystem it used to support itself. Sitting in David Geffen's white-walled office, washed in classical music, with a gorgeous painting staring down at me and David completely relaxed in blue jeans and a white t-shirt, was a lesson all of its own: At least one person had succeeded in the realization of this sort of life and career.

If him, why not me? Gerry Laybourne had been a schoolteacher before she founded Nickelodeon, and her office looked like the kind of space an enormously talented 12-year-old would be utterly content in. That space was a book, really, about the power of believing in what interests you.

John Hendricks had been a teacher, too, of public school biology students, which may explain why he could see the potential in an idea that the mighty National Geographic Society was rejecting almost simultaneously with his own humble launch of the Discovery Network. When I first visited John, he was holed up in a grim office in a grimmer suburb of the nation's capital. When I came back a year later, he was just settling into a showcase Bethesda, Maryland, office building with waterfalls and the sort of wonderful wildlife carvings that you would expect of a leading media brand. Like Gerry Laybourne, John had fed off his past experience to slip into his new dreams.

When Nancy Evans and I were thinking about creating iVillage, one of our first stops was the Motley Fool, the quirky online investment site that had turned traditional financial advice on its head. The group's headquarters is in Alexandria, Virginia, not far from where I had worked at Time-Life only six years before. There were other rising online media brands—Sportsline in Atlanta, for instance, and Cnet in Silicon Valley—but there was something appealingly off center about David and Tom Gardner, the brothers who had started Motley Fool.

To get there, we hopped a shuttle from New York and hired a car service to take us the short distance from National Airport to Alexandria—standard travel procedure for the corporate worlds we were both departing—but we were careful to have the driver park well out of sight of the townhouse that then served as the Fool's ground zero. Nancy and I were in our early-to-mid forties, already borderline for new-media pioneers. We didn't want to queer the session before it began by showing up in what we sensed might be politically incorrect transportation. [Three months later, as he handed us our seed money to start iVillage, AOL's Ted Leonsis (essentially, our godfather), would comment, "I think you might be too old, but . . . ." But, indeed, adult supervision and judgment came to be seen as valuable even in the Internet world.]

Inside the Motley Fool's townhouse was a three-room operation that looked nothing like any company we had ever seen: blank walls covered with poster boards filled with taped-on diagrams, a fake-wood conference table surrounded by spindly chairs holding maybe 15 young men, all of them ferociously, terrifyingly bright. We sat down and began to ask hundreds of questions: How do you do this? Who runs that? When and where does this get done? The answers were useful. We didn't know what an information systems manager might even look like, and as we would find out later when the first one we hired shushed us off the server we were sitting on to eat lunch, we didn't know much about what equipment he needed, either. But it was the space we were in, not the words, that began to give us the picture.

From that picture would come the aesthetic of our own space: Poster boards soon covered the walls in Nancy's basement. From the picture would come, too, the first space iVillage officially occupied: the first floor of a building in a no-name neighborhood that our partner Robert Levitan discovered, a space utterly devoid of charm. Even the better space we soon found—a beautiful little building with a gold dome in Lower Manhattan's Flatiron District—leaned heavily on the principle of space egalitarianism that we had first seen at the Motley Fool. When six of you are crammed into a tiny room, it doesn't matter whether you're the CEO, the CIO, a temp, or the mail clerk. If you get up to go to the bathroom, you will lose your seat.

Mostly, though, what Nancy and I got from that Motley Fool meeting was the confidence that we could start a network that eventually would attract more than 10 million women a month and $250 million in funding, and become one of the top 25 Web destinations worldwide. What the ferociously bright young men who sat around the table with us got from our time together, I can't begin to say. But we drank their blood, we smelled their air, we took it all in, and truth told, it was great.

Unedited Desires

One of the great benefits of understanding your stirrings is that you now can begin to assess just how close you are to where you want to get—whether it's being CEO of a Fortune 500 company, owning a baseball team, starting the next Cisco Systems, overseeing the dispersal of millions of dollars to causes you deeply believe in, teaching, acting, or staying at home for five years while the children grow into grade school. When our stirrings are pure abstraction, anything and nothing are equally possible. As we refine them and prepare to take them out into the world, we'll begin to find the holes in our dreams and in our own experience. In between, it's critical to give the process as much time to develop as you possibly can afford, financially and emotionally.

Rush through this stirrings phase, and you're most likely to edit your own desires: I can't do this, so I'll settle for that. This is out of my reach, so I won't go there. The truth is you don't know enough yet about where you are headed to know what is achievable; you haven't given the world the time or opportunity to rearrange itself in your favor. Like an anxious spring gardener, you're setting your seedlings outside before they've had a chance to develop the root structure they need to grow thick and strong. Only by refusing to edit your desires at this point can you ever unlock the full potential in them. Only by taking your stirrings and dreams with utter seriousness no matter what might seem the obvious obstacles can you give them the time and encouragement to grow into the real world.

> Assume you can. The first job of this stage is also one of the very hardest of the entire process: You need to learn not to edit your desires.

There's a reason people who go for what they want do better, John O'Neil told me: They are willing to work harder to make it happen. There's another reason, too: They refuse to put a cap on their dreams.

No one has captured this idea better than Robert Fritz, in his classic work *Creating*. Fritz was teaching music composition at the New England Conservatory when he became intrigued by why some students composed more successfully than others. External factors such as a good ear or the capacity to perform on an instrument or even time spent at the job didn't appear to explain the disparity. Nor did the usual measures of intelligence. Some students were simply better than others. Why?

Fritz took his question to friends who taught psychology and learning theory at Harvard, to no avail. Finally, he launched a multiyear study of his own that led to what might seem some counterintuitive answers. The key to achieving, he found—a great symphony, a great job, a successful life, even the little material rewards that successful lives can bring—lies in learning not to edit our desires. To a mediocre composer, a note is a problem, from its first formative moments. To a great composer, every note, from its moment of ideation, is alive with possibility. The difference is enormous.

By way of illustration, let me retreat to the trivial and my own life again. (I'm really not all about shopping, though I do regard its pleasures with gender-based reverence.) The other day I found myself at a Midtown Manhattan Mercedes dealership, looking at used cars. I happen to like used Mercedes. I've owned them for decades, usually very old ones that require tons of care and feeding. This time I knew exactly what model I should buy: a used station wagon, something appropriate to the single mother of two young girls that I had become. I was just about to sign for one—a very nice silver mommy-mobile with lots of room, all the appropriate safety features, nice resale potential, blah, blah, blah (the blahs were a clue)—when my eye happened to fall on a little silver convertible that didn't have a single blah attached to it.

That evening, a good friend of mine read me the riot act: There were the girls, of course (although four people can fit in a convertible, especially when two of them are still pretty tiny). There was the whole mommy thing. It was time to act like a grown-up. And so on and so on. In truth, I heard barely a single word she said. I knew where my desire lay, and I knew beyond a doubt that if I started editing the small desires, the large ones were going to begin to tumble over in a series of compromises that I might never recover from. Besides, the girls love the car—even seven-year-olds prefer sexy over staid—and if I have to work a little harder because it's a two door or because the top is down when a sudden storm comes up, I'm completely cheerful because this is the car I love. Even better, it was cheaper than the dull wagon. An economy measure! And one with a nice payoff. The other day in one of those beautiful bursts of springtime, I picked Michaela up from school and took her for a burger on Madison Avenue. Afterward, I showed her the flop-over method for getting in a convertible without opening the doors, and we worked on it until she had it just right.

A car is a car, not a life, unless your life needs serious work. But our dreams are polestars: They give us a light to plot our course by, and in plotting that course, we begin to arrange everything around it. And what applies to cars and the other peripherals in our lives has to apply with far greater force to the place where we're going to put our true energies for 60 hours a week or more. Edit your professional desires, and they, too, will begin to drown in compromise.

Don't get me wrong. There's plenty of tough work ahead if you're going to convert your stirrings into something lasting and real. In commenting on this same rough period in his own transition, Bill Bridges wrote, "One day I was ready to launch a new life, and the next I was bitterly suspicious of the motives of my supporters and my own promptings. 'What am I trying to prove?' I would ask. 'My life's not so bad as it is.'"

This is yo-yo time, which is why a great Navigator right now can be worth his weight in gold. There are people in your life who will by their very nature encourage your stirrings: Take time to think about who they might be. And there are people who won't be encouraging, not because they don't like you or love you or care about you, but for all the reasons we talked about before: They have a stake in who you were and are, and they're scared about the dislocation in their own beings that might be caused by who you are becoming.

But the larger point Robert Fritz makes applies here, too. When we really allow ourselves to want something and when we pursue it without editing our desires, something gets unleashed. Even if we don't have the least idea how to get what we want or how to create it if it doesn't yet exist, molecules begin to rearrange themselves around us, in our favor. Time and again when I've talked to people who have created truly great things, in themselves or for themselves or in the world at large, they've told me how the power of their intention itself was enough to move whatever mountains blocked the way.

The movie *October Sky* is about this same transforming quality of desire. There's no reason under the sun why four high schoolers from a West Virginia coal-mining town should succeed in their quest to build a rocket and use it to win college scholarships in a national science contest. The time was the late 1950s, the Sputnik era. The public schools of Appalachia offered little by way of quality, or even adequate, science instruction. The four boys were competing against the best and brightest from some of the swankiest schools in the land. Yet so deep and pure is their desire that it rallies the entire hardscrabble town to their cause and ultimately makes their dreams come true—in both the movie and the real-life story the movie is based on. If you ever find yourself doubting the quality of desire to move mountains, rush out and rent the video. Wanting something—truly wanting it—changes everything.

"Inherent in every intention and desire is the mechanics for its fulfillment," Deepak Chopra writes. "When we introduce an intention in the fertile ground of pure potentiality, we put this infinite organizing power to work for us."

I've been there. In the early days of iVillage, we had a sense of these forces. Yes, we worked 70-hour weeks. Yes, I was pulling two all-nighters a week just to keep up. But powerful forces that I still can't adequately explain were awakened by the force of our belief and desire. Obstacles that should have been immovable disappeared like a lifting fog. Objectives that should have been unobtainable by the usual rules of commerce—a place where millions of women could congregate and the most blue chip of advertisers would be proud to show their wares—simply happened. And they happened, I'm convinced, because we dared to want them to happen with all our being.

One example: Our goal at iVillage had been to line up four blue-chip, Fortune 500 sponsors before we launched. Like other media companies, our revenues would come through advertising relationships, but we wanted to forge those relationships early on, before we ever went online, so that we could create a deeper dialogue between their brands and the women who came to us. No one in our position had ever managed to do that, and at $250,000 a deal, we weren't offering our space cheap. With one week to go before launch, no one had signed on the bottom line, and then in one remarkable string, Robert Levitan signed up Toyota, Polaroid, MGM, and Starbucks, and suddenly we had hit the $1 million mark. Our desire had unleashed the mechanics for its fulfillment—nothing else can explain it.

Most of us trust these intuitive processes in product development or creative work: A great plot or software idea or symphonic movement leaps into our brain because we've lived for weeks in the possibility. It's time to learn to fully leverage those same processes in the expression of our careers. Done right, what we do, not what we make, can be the most creative act of all.

I had a wonderful guy in my living room the other evening: Jason Stell, the son of Loren Stell whom I had mentioned earlier. Now in his thirties, Jason had made his reputation running public relations for one of the glamour dot-coms. After taking time out to discover what his new stirrings were, Jason had stopped by to report on what he had found. He wanted to be an organizational development consultant, he told me, or maybe a psychiatrist. The final touches were waiting to be put on his dream, but he knew the direction now. His stirrings were talking to him, and he really, deeply wanted to go where they were leading him. His old friends and colleagues, though, were fighting him. He had hit a home run before in public relations—just mashed the ball over the fence—and they wanted him to do it again.

I told Jason that he needed to get out at this stage and expose himself to new threads, new lines of thought, new people. The bookstore or the local library isn't a bad place to start: Wander down the aisles, let your hot-cold beeper guide you, and don't edit your desires. When you find a title alive with possibility, buy it. The book might lead somewhere you never knew you wanted to go.

Get away from your old network also, I said, or you'll end up just where you are now, trapped in the projections of people who don't want to and maybe can't afford to hear about the person you are becoming. To help Jason get started, I put him in touch with Chris Ogden, who is already halfway through the transition Jason is about to embark on. That's how we can serve our friends in this new world: Get them hooked up with someone who chose the path they are contemplating, who has been over the worst of the hurdles and thinks life is one great ride. My reaching out to Jason's father put him back in touch with me. My reaching out to Chris put Jason in touch with him. My guess is that Chris will put Jason in contact with someone else, and that person with someone else still. These connections can go on and on because they are so organic, and as the web spreads, the seeming miracles can multiply.

A few years after my daughter Michaela was born, I went to a tiny town in Hungary, intent on adopting a sister for her. Five days later, I was ready to come home, defeated. What I had thought would be a charming rural hamlet was a concrete Eastern Bloc village with inedible food. No one spoke a word of English. (I was hitting the inevitable McDonald's when I needed a healthy meal and a scrap of English.) The foster parents of the little girl I had come for clearly despised me. Winter was on us. That evening, on what I expected to be my last night in the town, I went online in iVillage and told whoever was willing to listen that I was packing it in unless anybody had anything to say. The next morning, I had six e-mails waiting for me, six beautiful testimonials from women who had endured horrible odds to adopt the children they loved. Within a week after that, the formal adoption papers had been signed and my daughter and I were living in a Budapest hotel, waiting to fly home. This caring network I had coinvented—my little, loving iVillage—had given me six angels, six Navigators, when I most needed them, and those six strangers had guided me to the far shore and changed my life and the life of my little girl forever.

CHAPTER SIX

A Stake in the Ground

*You say yes, and I say no. You say stop,
and I say go, go, go . . . .*

—**The Beatles**

*I*t's time to take your dreams out into the world, time to expose this whole process of reinvention you've been going through to the light of day. David Zelman urges his clients to think of their stirrings as the branches of a tree (see page 136): Some will wither, some will be sent flying by ice or storms, but at least one branch will have to prove robust enough to shoot up toward the sun. That's the branch you're seeking, the one that will become your new life.

If you're heading out into the world still looking for a generic opportunity—I want to make lots of money, I want to find a fun place to spend my days—this part is going to be brutal. There are so many ways to accomplish such broad goals that the possibilities all begin to short-circuit one another. Eventually, you end up chasing your own tail. But if you're coming out into the world with a specific desire, if you've cus-

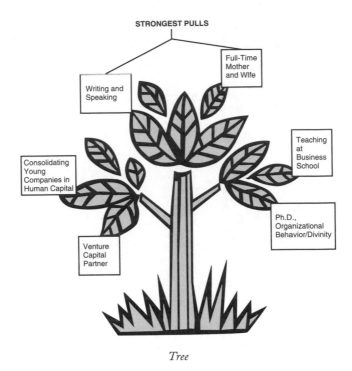

STRONGEST PULLS

Full-Time Mother and Wlfe

Writing and Speaking

Teaching at Business School

Consolidating Young Companies in Human Capital

Ph.D., Organizational Behavior/Divinity

Venture Capital Partner

Tree

tomized your dreams to your own uniqueness, then you're in for a very good time. That's why the walk in the desert is so important. There's a reward for specificity, a reward for taking the time to do this right, and this is the time to claim it.

Remember the lesson of "smart" bombs: They're effective because they seek to do only one thing at a time and know exactly where they should go to do it.

I was talking with a woman the other day who had left a white-collar job at Coca-Cola to raise her family. When the last of her children reached elementary school, she went back to work as a human resources consultant. Along the way, she had come to read extensively in the popular and professional literature of holistic medicine. It was an intellectual interest, nothing else, she said, but the more she thought about it, the more she made a connection in her own mind with assisted-living centers. Holistic medicine seemed to have so much to offer older people in terms of diet and exercise, and yet no one was carrying the message to the places where so many senior citizens were living.

She devised a plan that would have doctors volunteering five hours a week to visit assisted-living centers, tell staff members about the latest research in diet and exercise, and help them figure out ways to implement new programs that might revitalize the residents. On paper, it sounded great. In practice, she said, she thought she would be lucky if 1 in 20 of the doctors she approached agreed to take part. In fact, 175 of the 200 doctors she approached agreed to participate. She knew what she wanted, and knowing it helped make it happen.

Every time I've come out into the world with a powerful intimation of what I want to do next, I've found that it creates a kind of force field around me. I don't necessarily have a title in mind or even a fully formed job description at this point. I'm not asking for work. But the more defined my dream is when I begin to take it public, the more focused my research can be and the more organic the process becomes. One contact leads to another. Instead of fighting for face time, you find yourself part of a new circle of like-minded people. Ideas start to fly around, and as that happens, opportunities begin to stick to you like iron shavings to a magnet.

I was still at Time Warner Inc. when I had the first stirrings of the intuition that would become iVillage. It came during a group brunch when someone asked me what I wanted to do. "I want to create a media company," I answered, "one that has a brand based on demographics." In fact, I had no idea what that really meant—the words just came out of my mouth—but in October 1994, after I left Q2, Karen Quinn came over to my house with a blank sheet of paper and began asking me questions about my future. Within several hours I had taken that 1991 statement and given it a rudimentary shape and form. I still didn't know the audience would be the Internet. (I barely knew what the Internet was then!) But my stirrings were gaining force, and as they did, a magnetic field was forming around them. Another six months on, in May 1995, Nancy, Robert Levitan, and I sat around my dining room table and just made iVillage up. I pulled out the photograph just the other day—the three of us inventing a company because no model for what we wanted to do existed and because by then we could see with a clarity that still astounds us exactly what iVillage would become, exactly what it is today. A week later, Ted Leonsis told us that AOL wanted to back me in starting a media company. (Ted was the force of nature who foresaw the day when regular people would make the Internet a part of their lives.) This is what happens. There are more good matches in this world than we can ever imagine until we begin to seriously pursue them. Then, we're likely to be knocked over by all the seemingly chance connections that are, in fact, not chance at all.

Even when you have nothing more than a strong instinct about what you want to do next, this is the time to grab hold of it and begin to hone it. At iVillage, especially during the salad months of 1999 when everything was skyrocketing, we had a cadre of young, talented, and extraordinarily restless players. They knew what business they wanted to be in, and they knew where they wanted to fit into it—near or at the top. Their stirrings were close to complete. Their interests were in line, and their motivation, too. Many of their friends were starting companies of their own or being recruited to serve as the baby-faced CEOs of the rash of similar new-media companies that were pouring off the drawing boards, watered by a venture-capital flow that was reaching flood stage. If them, they were all asking themselves, why not me?

To keep these stars and to assuage their guilt about staying put (strange but true, for these were strange times), we worked with them to identify their drop-dead dream jobs and to understand the 20 skills that were most necessary to do those jobs well. Twenty was an arbitrary number; I picked it to show that great aspirations require a complex skill set. Many of our best young people were suffering from the idea that it was easy to get where we were trying to help them go. Once they had been through this process, we had each of them get feedback from their peers on which of those 20 skills they had actually mastered, generally about a quarter of the total package required since these were young people in a young industry. Next, we identified what job they could now take on at iVillage to help acquire as many of the missing skills as possible in as narrow a time frame as could be achieved.

I'll get into the details of this plan later, in Chapter 10, because I think this is something every company is going to need to pursue if it wants to hold on to its best talent in a fluid work world. Suffice it to say for now that, suddenly, we had put our best people on a fast track that would move them exponentially closer to their dream job at the end of the road, with a map in hand for how to get the rest of the way. Good for them, and good for us.

Grace Park had gone to an Ivy League school for her undergraduate degree and, almost in spite of herself, had moved on from there to another Ivy League school, this time for a law degree. The law interested her, she told me, but she felt no particular calling to practice it. As the daughter of a South Korean politician, law school simply seemed the desirable place to land. After graduation, Grace had moved on to a high-paying associate slot with a much-admired New York firm, where her misery with the profession compounded. By the time I met her, she had, almost predictably, jumped ship long before she should have. Moved by a parallel desire to get involved with the media but without doing any of the due diligence her graduate schooling had trained her for, Grace had taken a very junior position at one of the TV networks.

Instead of earning $150,000 a year, Grace was now making $30,000 a year. Rather than spending long hours in dank law libraries researching precedents, she was spending long hours in dank projection rooms, doing menial tasks for associate producers in some cases her own age. On the whole, it wasn't a great trade up, but Grace had a great advantage. She now knew what cluster of interests appealed to her: the law, media, and business. Grace had gone about things all wrong, boomeranging around her interest cluster without giving much thought to the details of how she might get where she wanted to go, but at least she now had a blueprint in hand.

What should she do, Grace asked me, after I had addressed a panel with Charlie Rose on this broad subject of chapters and reinvention. She had walked up to me cold, as soon as the panel broke up, nearly in tears. Talk to people whom you want to be, I told her. You know who and what that person is now. You're just confused about how to get there. Identify people who have walked this path before, people who have spent time in law, time in media, time in business. Go see them and find out what they made out of this same circle of interests and motivation. You'll be surprised how varied the results are and how receptive the people will be. Grace did. She talked with lots of people, and she was every bit as surprised as I had predicted.

"I would call and say, 'If you have a job for someone with my background, I am very open to talking with you about it, but if you don't, I still would like to meet you because I think what you are doing is really interesting and I would like some guidance on how to navigate myself to where you are,'" Grace told me. "I had to call people multiple times, but when I got to see them, they were very responsive. People enjoy talking about their lives, and I think they also empathized with me. A lot of them had been in my shoes at one point in their lives.

"I think this period of introspection and of meeting all these people was probably the most rewarding experience I've ever had. It was like someone hit me with a big frying pan: Wake up! Realize that it doesn't all happen in one day. It doesn't happen because you are different or creative or artistic. It happens because you work hard and put your head down and have a true feeling about what you want to do."

After all the interviewing, Grace took a job with a new consulting company, founded by former partners at one of the blue-chip consulting firms. She expects to spend as many as five years there, mastering the business skills she lacks. From there, she'll put the finishing touches on her media training and maybe on her law background. Instead of trying to jump immediately into her future, Grace is on the 20-step program. I can't predict what she will end up doing, but I can say with conviction that she'll be good at it by the time she gets there and she will end up at her own personal bull's-eye.

Homework

Even though your dreams are driving you, it's the voice of pure reason that you should be listening to now. In this home stretch, you can begin to edit your desires because you're bringing your dreams and the existing world together. Think of this as a final field test: The rubber is about to hit the road.

Not long after Craig Cohon determined that he would leave Coca-Cola to launch what ultimately became Global Legacy, he pretty much locked himself in a room for a month and produced a 200-page mission statement. From there, Craig moved on to interviewing 200 people who had moved out of the corporate world into the philanthropic one. When the generic exploration was done, he interviewed 200 more people who had combined in very specific ways their interest in business with a new initiative in social venturing. All the time, Craig was putting a more and more exact face on where he was headed, what he was about to create, and how he would exist within that creation. What kind of office space would he need? What kind of support staff? What was reasonable for someone in his proposed position to expect to bring home a month? What would travel expenses be? With each wave of exploration, the resolution got sharper, the details more refined. By the time Craig walked physically into his new life, he was already living there in his own head.

I don't pretend to have Craig's patience or thorough-
ness—or his obsession with the number 200—but in my own
way, I'm creating the options out of which I will form my next
chapter. However we get here, what's important is that all our
choices are flowing out of our desires—nothing exogenous,
nothing generic. "When you come to the fork in the road,"
Yogi Berra once commented, "take it." Suddenly, even that
seems to make sense.

One more thing to keep in mind in this period of reason-
ableness: Make sure you know who you are, but don't over-
look where you are. The answer you're seeking might be right
under your nose. Barbara Taylor had worked her way up to a
senior position at Edelman, the worldwide public relations
firm, but increasingly, she found her heart drawn to philan-
thropy. Barbara had talked with a number of nonprofits and
was on the verge of quitting when she took her new constel-
lation of interests to her boss. Instead of showing her the door
or wishing her good luck, he created a new division at
Edelman devoted entirely to global nonprofits and made
Barbara its executive vice president. Do such outcomes happen often? More than you think.

Money

One of the things that absolutely intrudes at this point is
money. In the stirrings phase, you can and should ignore it.
Nothing causes us to edit our desires more quickly than fear
of financial failure. You're past that, though. Now you can
stare the money issue square in the face. You're in a position
to trade—to weigh the things you care about and choose the
ones you care about most. If you feel like you're really depriv-

ing yourself, you're making the wrong trade, or pursuing the wrong dream at this juncture.

My lawyer and his wife were telling me the other day about their own experience with such budgeting. He'd been in-house counsel with a major corporation, overseeing a $50 million litigation budget. When he left, worn out by corporate politics, he, his wife, and their three children were living in a 14-room apartment on Riverside Drive, prime Manhattan real estate with a nice view of the Hudson River. Fearful (as I was when I left iVillage) of absorbing too much change at one time, they decided to give themselves 12 months in the apartment while he set out to create the boutique firm he dreamed of founding. When the numbers didn't add up a year later, they sold their spacious apartment and moved into a five-room apartment.

"We were radically downsizing," his wife said, "but it didn't feel like it. We knew what we were sacrificing for. We knew where all this was headed. We just needed to give ourselves a greater margin so we could get there. After our big place, we were living all on top of each other, but it was one of the most fun times we had." And ultimately, one of the most rewarding. With the extra time they bought by cutting back, my lawyer had time to get his firm in place and hire the right people. When the firm took off, and it did, the family upsized again.

Michelle Smith, a financial adviser who specializes in people in transition, talks about this time as the "integration phase." Don't dismantle your life right away, Michelle tells her clients. Give yourself six to nine months. By then, you'll know what your new life is going to be like, and you can make your financial profile fit it. By then, too, the decisions you'll be making will be free of the heavy emotional content from your past life. It makes very little difference how much money her clients have when they walk in the door the first time, Michelle told me. Their fear about money is identical. It's only when they open their perspective about the future that they can get past the limits that money imposes on them.

Back when I was flying high along the crest of the Internet bubble, I bought a lovely country compound—a perfect place for a CEO to entertain, a place to found a family dynasty. Not long ago, I traded down from the compound to a cottage on the edge of the woods. I know where I'm headed. I know my life will be more unstructured. Rather than feel deprived by my shrinking real estate claim, I feel exhilarated by it. I've taken the debt load of the big compound and converted it to fuel for my new passions. A financial obligation that was rock-hard solid has become fluid. That's a step up, not down. Just as important, I'm in a place far more aligned with the essentials of my current life. The old place bordered on the baronial; there, I was lord of the manor. As I walked through the woods the other day at my new country home, counting deer, I found myself thinking that this is what I want my girls to remember: not the grandeur of the compound but the intimacy of the cottage. It feels just right. I'm in love with it.

Setting the Stake

After Craig Cohon had written his 200-page mission statement, after he had interviewed his first round of 200 people and then a second round of another 200, after he had taken on a temporary identity by helping plan a world economic summit, he hired his first two employees before he had landed his first dollar of funding. And with that Craig did what we all finally have to do if we're going to take the step from research into reality: He drove a stake in the ground.

For every option we create, David Zelman suggests, the answer is "we will" or "we won't," but it's not until we actually place the stake that we know for certain what the answer will be, and even then we're sometimes still in the dark. My friend who marked his boxes "A" and "B" during the office rehab was placing a stake in the ground as surely as Don Marrs was when he grew his beard. Both of them just had to take the time to see what they had done. The same is true of the brightly colored Hermes jacket I bought just as I was leaving Time Warner—a one-of-a-kind uniform that I now see symbolized my transformation from a corporate to an entrepreneurial world. Karen Quinn dyed her hair orange, red, and blond the week she knew her Amex days were over, as though to make sure she wouldn't jump from one corporate behemoth to another.

> We often commit ourselves unconsciously to a future through small gestures until one day we realize we have walked from the world of possibility into the space of commitment.

A stake in the ground is more complicated than quitting or firing ourselves. Quitting is what gets us out of who and what we were, our past life. Stakes in the ground are often the sum total of that past, but what's truly important about them is that they irrevocably commit us to the future—to something new, a different path, a fresh definition of self. These are stakes that mark births, not burials.

My friend Dan Lewis quit his job as an investment banker not long after scaling Mt. McKinley during a vacation with his brothers. Whatever he had seen and experienced at that height had been enough to tell him that a chapter of his life was over, but it took seven more months before he was ready to drive his own stake in the ground. In the meantime, to give himself an anchor while he walked the desert and listened to his stirrings, Dan had moved into an office offered by a friend, and together the two of them set out to buy a small business.

"It was the end of August. I remember I was in my office at my friend's firm, and we had a conference call, to be told from the seller of the business that someone else was going to buy it. He had offered more money, and we were not going to get it.

"I heard that. I hung up the phone, and basically, the second that I hung it up, I knew that I was moving to the West Coast and going into partnership with another good friend. He and I had, in fact, talked about it for four years. He had said, 'Come out to the West Coast. You'll like living here. We should be in business together.' But I was afraid to do it. I didn't want to leave the East Coast, and on and on and on.

"I had erected a series of artificial barriers to saying yes to that, but the moment I hung up the phone, I knew I was going to do it. I took a walk outside. It was a bright day in Connecticut, and I remember that I knew my life had just changed. I called my friend the next day and said, 'I'm coming.' That was late August. I sold my house and, in December, I moved."

Dan had gone into investment banking, he told me, "with the view that I would be somewhat of a counselor and trusted adviser. Over the 15 years that I was in the job, it became increasingly clear that I was more of a salesman. That was a different psychological contract. As I got to know my own personality, it became clearer and clearer, deep down inside, that there was a mismatch between my own personality and the job I was in." There was a boss, too, right at the end of his investment banking career who had been a bad match, at best. And there was the deal that had gone awry.

All that explains why Dan made the call—why he put down the stake he did, when he did— but the call itself wasn't about that: The call was about the new person being born out of all this experience, which is why we need to know as absolutely as we can who that person is before we drive the stake and also why stakes in the ground tend to cast us into a kind of limbo even when we do know. In our minds, we have been someone else for weeks, maybe even months and years, but now we are someone else in the world's mind, too, a far different proposition. For Dan, the state of limbo was almost literal.

You are not looking for a job—you are seeking a match in the outside world with what stirs you.

"One day, I woke up and all my stuff was on moving trucks, and I had no life left on the East Coast except for my family. All my stuff was in transit, and I had no life yet on the West Coast either. It was a very bizarre feeling that said, okay, now go out and build a life personally and professionally.

"It was scary, but I just felt like it was meant to happen and that I was executing against something that was meant to be. I wasn't going to let anything deter me. I was moving to the West Coast to create a business, and I'd gotten over my main fears that I couldn't do it. You know, I was in the swimming pool. I'd made the leap. Now the only thing left was to make sure I swam the length of the pool.

"After I made the call and said I was coming, I had a moment of disappointment. Then I had this kind of exhilaration. There's a Yiddish word, *bashert*, which means 'meant to be.' When two people get married, you could say, it's *bashert*; it was meant to be. That's what the move felt like to me. It was meant to be. It was a transforming time."

As one Yiddish scholar told me, *bashert* is always spoken with three parts affection and one part resignation.

We all proceed at our own pace. We all do it in our own way. But finally in so many of these stories there's a moment of what can seem at the time sheer recklessness, but which in fact makes all the difference. Not everything in life can be screwed down first. If you wait for the last *i* to be dotted and *t* to be crossed, life is likely to have moved on, and opportunity with it, and quite possibly your own real stirrings, too. Doing the research, performing due diligence on yourself, cuts down the odds of making a mistake, or putting the wrong stake down in the wrong place, but you can't stop letting the dreams and stirrings inform you. They're what you have at these moments of transition—your own most valuable asset.

Bob Kerrey was already into his reelection campaign in the spring of 2000—for what would have been an almost certain third term in the U.S. Senate representing Nebraska — when he got a call from a member of the board of the New School for Social Research in New York City.

"The call came from a very good friend on the board, Julian Studley. He said, 'We're looking for a president. I wondered if you have any ideas?' He came down to

Washington, and we talked. Not long afterwards, I called him back and said, 'Julian, for some reason I can't get your request off my mind. Are you thinking about me?' And he said, 'I was.' I told him I'd have to push it back a little bit. But I found myself more interested than I should have been, given that I'd started the reelection campaign. Finally, to deal honestly with both situations, I had to stop one and confront the other.

"I gave myself two weeks, not time off so much as just time to talk to people and give myself space to be quiet and think. I talked with good friends and supporters. What they said was important, but the process of allowing them to say something was more important. It told them that I cared about them, that I loved them, and that I valued their friendship and participation. At the end of the two weeks, I wrote a couple of statements. One said I was going to run; the other said I wasn't. And the one that said I wasn't made me smile from ear to ear so I knew it was the right thing. The next day I had a press conference and announced I wasn't going to run for reelection."

That was the first fork in the road, Bob told me—the decision of whether or not to leave public life. The second one, whether or not to take the presidency of the New School, was still uncertain, a risk for both him and the university. But risk is a large part of what this time is about, and until you take that first fork, the second can never be confronted. (Bob, in fact, said yes to the New School within days of announcing his resignation from the Senate.)

Chris Ogden packed up everything he owned and left for graduate school with no real idea at the time of where he would find the money to pay for his Ph.D. in therapy. Dan

Lewis jumped ship from the East Coast, moved to San Francisco with no contract, no job, with nothing more than a broad sense of what his new venture-capital firm would look and function like, then set about constructing the actual blueprint with his friend and partner once he got there because Dan, too, couldn't have done it any other way.

No matter how systematic you are, the final blind leap to commitment is apt to seem reckless and crazed. This is the way the world moves forward.

"We knew this wasn't going to be about stamping out deal after deal," Dan explained. It was going to be about people judgments, about creating a web of relationships that are mutually beneficial for people in the firm, for the company, for the investors, and for the resources of the firm. We knew that we were starting a network of our friends that was going to help entrepreneurs accelerate their progress. But what form any of that was going to take, we didn't know. The first three months of 1998, I fumbled around, saying 'What is our business model?'

"If you're going to build a hundred-story skyscraper, you'd better make sure the foundation is really well placed and the footings are perfect. That was where we were. Those first three months were an opportunity for me to really grapple with my own values, my own priorities, my own choices, and make sure that we had a core business model that was aligned with our core values and that it would stand the test of time. And it was important to do that right, because if you get it wrong the first time and it's not where you want to be, then a year or two or five years out, you are going to say, well, that's not really what I want, and you're going to be stuck."

With remarkable consistency, people talk about the trans-forming quality of this moment of driving a stake in the ground, how it can convert even bad news to good. After all the "Will I?"/ "Won't I?" you're finally committed for all the world to see. You've become.

Don Marrs tells about meeting a famous producer in Los Angeles and asking him if he could work with him for no money for six months. In the world Don was leaving, it was a thoroughly reasonable request: free labor in return for free tutelage. In the world he had just driven his stake into, he might as well have asked for 10 percent of gross. "Why would I want to train you?" the producer asked. "You'd just end up being one of my competitors."

"In one sentence, he had told me everything there was to know about the business," Don writes. "It was every man for himself, and the key was a hot property." You could spend four years in a university and learn less: Don gave up trying to find a job and wrote a script instead. As so often happens, even the people who rain on our parade have important lessons to teach us. My friend Karen Quinn has been planning a business called Smart City Kids that will help parents navigate the truly horrible process of getting their children into private schools in New York City. That sounds nuts, I know. But anyone who has tried raising chil-dren in the madhouse of Manhattan will understand. Karen called the other day to say that she had just field-tested the business with a prospective client who had told her, in effect, nothing personal, I would rather use one of your competitors, a consultant who has been in the business for decades. Should she give up the idea, Karen asked me? Well, I told her, it's always good to get the downside on the table, but if the competition is so great, why does the process still make all of us so neurotic and miserable? Two days later, Karen called back to say that one of the most important Manhattan private schools had committed to supporting her success, suggesting that the consultant who had been doing this for so long was no longer in touch with what schools have to offer today. Suddenly, her fear had evaporated, and she was light-years closer to realizing her goal.

As courageous as he is, Chris Ogden felt the same fear as he prepared to leave his New York career behind and move west to an unknown future.

"The more real it became, the more and more frightening it was," Chris told me. "What if I'm making the wrong decision? What if I go out there and this turns into financial suicide? What if I'm really doing this because I want to run away from what I'm doing? What if I'm a failure at it? This idea of going to graduate school in your fifties—I'd never been a success in school before. So, God, I mean, can I still learn?

"I went to see one friend a few times and just said, 'I am peeing in my pants. I am so frightened.' And as the days grew closer to the actual day the moving van was going to come, I was virtually panicked. What if I fail? What if I hate it? What if? What if? What if?"

When did the fear finally lift, I asked Chris after we'd been talking about all this for almost an hour.

"When the moving van left. Once it was done, it was over."

Commitment does that. It transforms. It takes seemingly impossible barriers of competition and tosses them aside. The more you get out in the world with your passion, the more

you examine the truth of things, the deeper your own determination grows. Often, you'll hit a critical mass where things
begin to happen of their own accord. A writer friend was
telling me recently about a train enthusiast he had just interviewed in South Florida. For a number of years, the train buff
had worked for an industrial paint company while his wife
held an executive position with a bank. When their daughter
turned two, they decided that he would step back and take
care of her until she was ready for full-time school. He had
the more stressful job; she, the larger salary; and besides, he
had his home shop, where he was constructing a narrow-
gauge steam engine, to keep himself occupied. Soon after he
left his job, the train enthusiast learned that a vintage 1920s
full-scale steam engine was for sale. Over six months, he and
a partner put together a plan to purchase the engine and
move it to the Miami-area railroad museum where he volun-
teered on weekends as chief engineer. By the time his daughter is in elementary school, he expects to have the engine
operational for charity dinner runs to benefit the museum,
and he fully expects to be occupying the engineer's seat himself. I can't tell you how many similar stories of almost har-
monic convergence I've come across while writing this book.
Once you begin looking for them, they are everywhere.

Just Say No

One of the most important lessons I've learned from David
Zelman is this: It's okay to say no. Most people get to yes too
quickly. Just at the edge of getting what they want, they settle
for less because it's what they can grab hold of. Barry Diller
dreamed of buying AOL. His year of trekking across America

told him in unmistakable terms what its future value would be. But before he could fully set his sights on AOL, Barry jumped when he was offered the chance to buy QVC. A bad idea? No, not at all. But Barry perhaps said yes a moment too soon, and he now lists not getting AOL as a major, and for him rare, regret.

Time and again just after I've left a chapter of my life, I've been offered incredibly prime opportunities to jump back into the fray before I was ready. This time has been no exception. Some of the offers are easy to reject: They're about what I was—CEO, media brands. I know I'm not going there again, at least not right now. Others are far closer to what I want to be because I've begun to place that person in play in the world. With David Zelman's help, I'm learning to hang out in "maybe" with such offers, not rejecting them out of hand but rather working with whoever has made one to see how close we can bring it to what I really want. It's not a matter of negotiating or making a counteroffer. I'm inventing a new chapter for myself, and I'm trying to fashion a place where this person I'm going to be can be most comfortable and successful. Until I get the fit, it's empowering to say no because the "no" I'm saying is an expression of forward commitment. Even better, when I do say yes, I'll mean it through and through.

> When you know what you want, you don't have to bargain. Saying a simple no to something that isn't a match can open the way to making it the match you want. This is different from negotiating.

John O'Neil, author of *The Paradox of Success* and perhaps the foremost contributor to our understanding of the high cost of great achievement, talks about such offers as pushing "the heroic button in you that 'you're the only person who can save them' or 'if you save us, then we'll do wonderful things in the world.' You've got to watch out for those messages because they burn you." He told me that he had responded to those several times, and they always are not good.

The call should be easy, but as John's own response suggests, it never is. Often, we're coming off warrior status. The temptation to turn around and put the armor back on before we've had a chance to get in touch with our deeper selves can be almost overwhelming. Saving things is what we've known, what's defined us to ourselves for maybe years on end. Other times, we know where we're going, but we're not quite ready to go there yet. Even with my new knowledge and a great Navigator, I'm still not totally immune to this summon to heroism. I went to a meeting with another company just the other day. I thought my role was going to be a bit part, but when I showed up, I was the one who was supposed to bring home the scalp. An acquisition was in the offing; having me at the top, if only for just a short while, would make the deal more attractive. I flicked the switch and put on the show that everyone present needed. At the end, the head guy turned to me and said, "Great. Go get 'em!" But all I wanted to do was take a nap. I had gone into the fray prematurely, without any of the enthusiasm we feel when we're ready for combat.

Randy Christofferson gets my all-time all-star award on this front. Randy had joined Bain, a consulting firm, in 1983 and immediately put in the 90 hours a week expected of those who wanted to make partner in a hurry. In time, he had been recruited to American Express to run its strategic planning. Before long, he was leaving the house at 4:30 in the morning, getting home at midnight, and putting in an hour or two more then. By the time he was 32, Randy had taken 10,000 people off the employment roles at Amex, squeezed out $1 billion in costs, and become one of the top dozen people in the entire company. For his reputation, it was great. For his life, it was far less so. He and his wife, Judy, were on their way to four children, and Randy was becoming a stranger to all of them.

To slow his life down, Randy agreed to become president of First USA, a bank he grew from 2,800 employees to 27,000. It all was going great, he told me, and then BankOne bought First USA. The deal made Randy comfortable financially, but it also tied him down. By the terms of the agreement, he had to stay two years. The money disoriented him, too. Finally, when the required time was up, several friends at the bank came to him and said, "Why are you here? We have to work, but you don't."

"I called my wife," Randy said, "and then I called my boss and quit that morning. I made the call at eleven, left the building at three, and I've never gone back inside it."

That's when temptation really walked in the door. On the eve of taking priceline.com public, Jay Walker approached Randy and offered him the job as CEO. iVillage and others had already pretty much set the market for such events: The math wasn't hard to do. Over two bottles of wine one night in their kitchen, Randy and Judy calculated that the deal would be worth $500 million, not only enough to make them super-rich but enough to provide for both their families even through the level of nephews and nieces and also to set up a foundation that Judy could make her life's work. Both of them, Randy said, were sobbing by the end of the night when he decided to turn the job down.

"I'd started a band with my friends and I was on a hockey team. It sounds crazy, but life — everyday life — seemed precious," Randy told me. "They were expecting me to come to Connecticut the next day and accept, and I got there and said, 'Listen, I just don't want to walk people around the block any more. I don't want to do all that slogging.' And Jay Walker said, 'You're right. You need something more cerebral.'" Priceline did go public, and even more spectacularly than Randy had anticipated: The deal would have been worth $700 million on paper. And, of course, priceline also went into the tank when the Internet bubble burst. Ultimately the deal would have been worth nothing. For his part, Randy also got what he wanted without ever having to ask for it. Jay Walker made him CEO of Walker Digital — closer to running a think tank than heading up a traditional company. What's more, Walker provided a helicopter that carried him to work everyday. When Walker Digital also succumbed to the Nasdaq collapse, Randy stopped leaving home every morning. Like me, he thought he had always been there for his children; after all, he was home every weekend. Now, he said, he gets to watch all of Andrew's lacrosse games. He can see him develop contest by contest — one of the pleasures of being able to dip into the texture of your kids' lives. Randy had seen a potential half billion dollars disappear in front of his eyes; instead of counting his money, he was worrying about how to keep alive the winning streak of the high school hockey team he had agreed to coach. Whenever I've seen him recently, he has seemed thoroughly content.

One last element of this "no-saying": Sometimes you have to be able to tell yourself the hard truth that a dream just isn't right for now. There's no crime in this, nor any failure.

The working world is by its very nature unstable. The terrain changes constantly. Even great ideas have to be put on hold when the fundamentals fall apart.

Joe Colivito had been in the executive search business for many years when he and a partner developed a software product that they were convinced would improve the quality of the matching process. Joe was so sure of the efficacy of the software that he and his wife agreed to devote a large portion of their nest egg to turning it into a business. When they had burned through the agreed-upon amount, they decided to dip further into their reserves to buy a few more months' time, but while they were doing that, the landscape was undergoing a radical reshaping. Nasdaq was crashing and burning. Start-up funding was running dry. Joe and his wife also had to factor in a fourth baby on the way. Finally, they agreed to put the idea on the shelf, and Joe went back to collecting a regular paycheck as a partner with Heidrich and Struggles. Had he failed to give his passion a run, I feel certain Joe would be disappointed with where he is today. But he did give his dream a run—he took the idea as far as it could go in the climate he had to deal with, and he was completely honest with himself at the end. Instead of wallowing in regret, Joe's enjoying his position. What's more, he's convinced that his idea isn't dead forever, just for the time being. In the meantime, he can look for still other ways to develop his passion for transforming the interview and selection process.

Later isn't never. Sometimes your homework will tell you a dream isn't possible for now, but delayed dreams often surface successfully in later chapters. With serial reinvention, nothing is wasted.

Take your stirrings out into the world without a clear sense of what you want to be next, and you'll just end up punching the clock for someone else's dream, no matter how well paid you are. Know who you are, know what you want to be next, do the tough due diligence on yourself and your ambition, and be honest at every step along the way even when the truth hurts, and whatever story line you end up in, it will be your own creation. That's the bottom line here. That's what makes all the difference.

CHAPTER SEVEN

Into the Zone

When you truly possess all you have been and
done, you are fierce with reality.

—Florida Scott-Maxwell

There's a scene that sticks in my mind: Nancy Evans, Robert Levitan, and I have embarked on our first fund-raising adventure for iVillage. Earlier, we had drummed up $2 million in seed money to put together an initial team and get the site up and running, which we did at the stroke of midnight on December 31, 1995, just as the new year was launched. Now, we are setting out to raise $10 million more to carry us through the next 12 months of expanding the site, our brand, and our advertiser base. We had all been around big money for years, but none of us had ever gone out and asked for it like this. We'd worked for weeks on the presentation: in our new office, in Nancy's basement, in my apartment, wherever one or two could gather. For weeks, too, we had been eating steak at nearly every meal—for breakfast, for lunch, for dinner, for all those weird times in between when you don't have any idea what to call a meal but that occur with ever-greater frequency in times like these. Nancy is no great carnivore. I'm practically a vegetarian by now, but steak it was, nice and bloody.

Already, we've taken our road show to the Tribune Company, Liberty Media, and a few other high-quality firms. Basically, we are giving people the right to abuse us day and night in return for their cash. Now we've come to the plutonium core of the New Economy: Kleiner Perkins, the venture group that has funded Amazon and Excite, to only scratch the surface. A few hours earlier we had flown into San Francisco by coach. A car service has brought us out to Sand Hill Road in Silicon Valley. Now, with only minutes to go before what could be one of the most important meetings of our lives, Nancy and I—two women of high style, refugees from a world where propriety counted greatly—are standing on the macadam behind our limo in the Kleiner Perkins parking lot, changing out of our blue jeans.

Did we mind? Did we mind the yet-another-steak we had after the presentation? Did we mind the overnight red-eye we caught home later that night: more grim overnight coach seats in two lives that had graduated to daytime flights and business class almost from the moment business class had been born? No, not at all. We were in the Zone—the magical place I would wish for every professional life, where time stands still because we are living so completely in the moment and loving every second of it, even the seconds we hate. It didn't hurt either that before we touched down in New York the next morning, we had $10 million in the bank that Robert Levitan could use as evidence of our credibility so he could sign the very first sponsors that helped to launch a Web-based network where millions of women would congregate.

Trying to describe the Zone is like trying to describe the thrill of great sex or a spectacular sunset seen from an unbelievable perch in a mountain range you barely knew existed or the instant inundation of the senses that comes from a first sip of Dom Perignon or the first explosion of true beluga caviar on the tongue. It can be done, but unless you're James Joyce or Jan Morris or Molly O'Neill, it sure isn't easy.

Bob Kerrey came the closest to getting it right, I think, when he was describing for me his heady first years as a United States Senator: "Everything works, even the things that don't work. You don't want to go to sleep at night, and you can't wait to get up in the morning." The Zone consumes you almost without your knowing it. It eats up your energy and draws forth new reservoirs of fuel you had no idea existed.

In the Zone, deprivation, inconvenience, and exhaustion go unnoticed in the name of what you truly desire.

Next, Not Biggest or Again

The Zone is not about repetition. For all the blows life has dealt high-flying financier turned entrepreneur Michael Milken and all the ones he has inflicted on himself, Milken always moves on to a new chapter—from global finance to spearheading funding for prostate cancer research to launching Knowledge Universe and turning it almost overnight into the dominant player of the for-profit education sector.

Considering that he passed through prison along the way, it's been a remarkable run. More important, it's a run that always ends Milken up in a new Zone. Cancer or not, jail or not, Milken remains alive with possibility. For all the blows life has dealt John deLorean, the revolutionary and flamboyant automaker, and all his self-inflicted ones, deLorean always goes back to making cars, and thus having once found the Zone with his gorgeous gull-winged eponymous deLorean, he has never found it again. The difference is profound.

None of that means you can't find the Zone time and again within a single field or under the aegis of a single employer. It means only that repetitive ambitions dull the spirit and steal energy in the same way that repetitive tasks numb the body and dull the mind. The U.S. Army's up-or-out policy at the officer rank can be brutal, but a well-lived Army career can be a succession of Zones within a single uniform. Whether he was serving as a White House Fellow under Caspar Weinberger and Frank Carlucci in the early 1970s, as military adviser to Secretary of Defense Weinberger in the mid-1980s, as National Security Adviser in the last year of the Reagan administration, or as chairman of the Joint Chiefs of Staff under George Bush in the late 1980s and early 1990s, or just punching his ticket at various military postings along the way, Colin Powell lived fully in the moment of what he was doing. His energy was palpable, and still is as Secretary of State, and that energy has a transforming quality, not just for Powell but for everyone around him.

Nor is the Zone about always topping your last life. Think of each chapter as trumping the previous one—more money, more fame, more votes, more clout—and you'll never escape the centrifugal pull of all the previous life segments you have

led. Instead of reinvention, you'll spend your days score keeping, and probably score settling. One long-time friend has
been running a hedge fund for years. He admits that he takes
no pleasure from the work; all that keeps him going, he says,
is the prospect of topping his last year's return, his previous
five-year return, and so on. In effect, he's stuck in a contest
with himself that only death or complete failure can end.
Worse, by definition, he's outside the Zone.

I left mountaineering without ascending El Capitan,
the great Yosemite rock face that is often considered the
crowning achievement of American climbing. Could I have
done it? Yes, I feel certain, but it would have taken another
two years of training, especially weight training, to prepare.
El Capitan is not for the weak or the faint. And once I had
climbed it, what would I have been faced with? The search
for another crowning achievement. Like the bear who went
over the mountain, there's always another mountain waiting
just ahead. If reinvention is your goal, at some point you have
to step off the trail, no matter how high or far it's taking you.
Besides, I know now what it was impossible for me to
know then: More than 20 years later, not a soul in the world
cares whether I made the El Capitan ascent or not—especially not me.

One more case in point, and a lesson learned painfully.
One of the earlier executive hires we made at iVillage was a
man who came from a large corporation. His credentials were
excellent, but I should have paid more attention to the questions he kept asking: What size would his office be? Who
would be doing the decoration? How about title and salary? In
retrospect, I can see that he was trying to have his new chapter carry all the status weight from his old one—we were a

start-up, not Time Warner—but all I could see then was that we were filling a key slot. Not surprisingly, he never performed, never did well, never slipped into the Zone that nearly everyone else at iVillage was living in.

Like novels, lives have rising action and falling action, moments of grand intrigue and epic consequence interspersed with other moments of calm steadiness, quiet accomplishment, little acts that bind the whole and complete its texture, and sad, even tortured episodes without which we would never know when the good times arrive. That's the life this book prepares you for: not one of ever-widening gyres, ever-greater spheres of influence, but one in which the parts fit together with a natural harmony. Others can rank the success of your chapters; only you can rate the fulfillment they have brought you, individually and collectively. The Zone is what happens when we live in the realization of our deepest stirrings, each of them, wherever each might lead us, whatever size and shape they might assume.

A college friend had been diagnosed with cervical cancer in her early thirties. Eighteen months ago, in her late forties, the cancer returned. A grinding bone marrow transplant was her last hope. When that failed, her doctor told her to get her affairs in order. Instead, my friend quit her job with a data nationwide moving company and used part of the savings she had set aside for her old age to buy a home for the son who had left his job to tend to her when she came home from the marrow transplant. For over a year now, she has been using much of the rest of her savings to travel the world—twice to the Caribbean to scuba with her son and his partner, once to Southeast Asia with her sister, once to Argentina with a childhood friend.

When I talked with her by phone not long ago, she sounded great. Whatever medicine she was on worked well "most of the time," she said. She had no illusions that she was out of the woods. Short of a miracle, she's writing the last chapter of her book, but what a chapter it is. Even at the end, it's possible to live completely in the Zone, fully in the heart of our desire. It's all a matter of what we tell ourselves in our private conversations. Maybe, too, the transforming power of desire has given her time she wouldn't otherwise have had.

The Path of Least Effort

Bill Strickland operates in the Zone as a matter of course, whether he's flying jets or building and running his Manchester Craftsmen's Guild. Ask him the secret of his multiple successes, and he's inclined to talk about the effort he puts into each of them.

"I'm resourceful and I don't sleep much, so I have a big advantage over most people because I'm working much harder than they are. I sleep maybe four or five hours a night. While other people are sleeping, I'm thinking, What's my next move? How can I do this? That gives me a real competitive advantage."

But Bill also exemplifies one of the strange paradoxical qualities of the Zone. The harder you work to bring something you truly desire to fulfillment and the more unrelenting you are in being true to your dreams, the more you bring your talents and aspirations into alignment. And the more you do that, the more things just happen in a strangely effortless way.

Housed in a Frank Lloyd Wright building in a once elegant inner-city neighborhood, the Guild is a center for community kids and their parents unlike any other in America and maybe in the world. Rather than settle for cast-off institutional furniture, Bill insists on top-of-the-line ergonomic chairs, and on desks and worktables that are right for whatever they're being used for—painting, ceramics, metalwork, you name it. The first thing kids see when they enter the building are fresh orchids—fresh every day, grown in a greenhouse just constructed on the site. Not only do Manchester kids get to look at the orchids; they also learn how to grow them. In the same spirit, Bill includes under the roof a gourmet-quality cooking school so kids can learn a trade that they can follow to ownership and so that the school cafeteria will serve food as good as the setting. Not long ago, he added a 9-foot Steinway grand piano to the mix.

The idea behind it all is a grand extension of the art room Bill studied in and the art teacher he studied under in high school. The center is meant to be "a permanent structure" for lives that have been filled with impermanence—"a place," he says, "that people can count on, a place they can be in as long as they live and that will never go away." Beyond that lies an even larger and more important idea: The flowers, the gourmet food, the art and crafts that decorate the halls, the jazz that floats through the building are "over time the cure for spiritual cancer. The sunlight, the quilts, the beauty—they bring people back to life." Kids, in short, often become their environments. Surround them with secondhand furniture and they'll develop secondhand minds and second-rate ambitions. Treat them to beauty and class, though, and they'll dream beautiful dreams that they can walk into and become a part of. Who you think you can be makes all the difference in who and what you become.

A few years back, Bill got a call from jazz legend Herbie Hancock, who had heard about the center and wanted to have a look for himself. That meeting led to a parade of concerts at the center by nearly all the living jazz greats. Like Herbie, many of them donated one of their original recordings to the organization—the center now boasts the world's largest single collection of unpublished jazz, a profit center as well as another way of surrounding the people who train there with creative beauty. It was Herbie Hancock, too, who provided the impetus for taking Bill Strickland's dream national and maybe even global. When Hancock expressed an interest in building a West Coast version of the center in San Francisco, his friend the mayor arranged for the donation of 5 acres of waterfront property for the purpose.

> Because strong forces are magnetized to your causes, you will experience surprising incidents of effortless grace.

The energy released in the Zone has an almost exponential quality. It's its own form of higher-plane networking: Mission attracts mission, talent attracts talent, aspiration attracts aspiration until what can seem from the outside and even from within to be hard labor becomes something else entirely: a kind of organic effortlessness that can move mountains and dig deep into the texture of lives.

"We've never had one fight at the center," Bill Strickland says. "No drugs, no alcohol, no theft, no racial incidents. How does that happen? It happens because the students are communicating the culture to the next generation coming into the place, long before they get there. That's powerful, powerful stuff."

In March 1999, when iVillage's chief financial officer and I were getting ready to take our company public, we criss-crossed the nation in a two-week road show that took our case directly to major investors. I'd practiced for the previous two weeks to get the presentation just right, and once I had my end down, I stuck with it come hell or high water: two cities and up to seven presentations a day, eighty presentations in all during that transcontinental tour. Nights were spent in wherever the local Hyatt was, always with an eye to the next day's grind. Between shows, I was living on Hershey bars and Diet Pepsis. The red-meat craze of my earlier money-raising tour disappeared until the last evening of the road show: Just as we were leaving Philadelphia to head for home, we stopped the hired car and ordered cheese steaks, two for me.

The trip was both mind-numbing and body-leveling, as innately miserable a two weeks as I ever hope to spend, and the truth of the matter is that I never once minded the repetition or the tedium or the horrible meals or the Hyatt nights because I was in the Zone: completely committed to the mission of our company and to completing this essential milestone.

Not long ago, my driver was talking about all the times during those iVillage years when he would pick me up at 5 a.m. to begin the workday and return me home after midnight. None of it surprised me. In the beginning, the notion of iVillage had been an abstraction, nothing I was ready to bet the ranch on, much less alter my life dramatically to achieve. But once the idea got its hooks in my heart, once my desire and its achievement became inseparably intertwined, there was no stopping either it or me. Deadlines, all-nighters (lots of them), funding crises, personnel crises, customer crises, weeks and weeks of truly bad food—not only did they not matter; I never even noticed that they were supposed to make me miserable.

I like to look good. I like to get made up. There have been chapters in my life when the right lipstick, the right everything mattered deeply to me. I'm a girl. Yet one evening when I was in the iVillage Zone, the then love of my life showed up for a date. I answered the door in a flannel bathrobe with my hair wet and piled on top of my head. "You know what," I said to him, "if you could just come back in five years . . ." and he walked away and married someone else. And even that didn't seem strange. Relationships in the Zone are of a different order and magnitude, so intense and transcendent that when I leave the Zone, I often have trouble recognizing the people I knew and worked with while I was there. One friend says that while he was in the Zone, people would come up to him in restaurants and ask if he was a celebrity, a movie star; there was a radiance, a glow to him that they could feel. When you are in the Zone, time compresses: Days pass as minutes, weeks as hours, years as months. You have guardians. Whether it's a backdraft, a magnetism, or some form of divine intervention, things fall in place, life organizes itself, all the atoms know where to gather. As Bill Strickland learned, there's an effortlessness that comes with such huge and hugely focused exertion, an exponential multiplier effect that takes human labor and makes it seem almost superhuman.

Recently, I listened to a panel of leading global CEOs discussing the modern corporate chief executive. Was it even possible any more to do a great job as the role becomes ever-more demanding and complex? The head of a German bank knew exactly how he felt: The job was different, yes, but only in degree, not kind. It could of course be done well, although maybe more time was required than would have been necessary a generation ago. Another CEO, this one a doctor of psychology as well as a student of the fine arts, wasn't so certain. Leadership wasn't top down any longer, he noted; it had to surface from all points on the corporate compass. What did control even mean in such a structure? Then a recently retired chief executive officer broke in with words I remember clear as a bell: "You know," he said, "I loved being CEO, but since I stepped down a few months ago, I also love not being CEO."

That's exactly what the Zone is like. When you are in the Zone, you're a warrior: never tired, rarely discouraged, utterly focused on winning, on conquering, on bringing home scalps on behalf of your tribe. There's a logical consistency to everything you do, every sacrifice you make that disappears almost the moment you leave the space. Once outside the Zone, it's almost impossible not to look back and think to yourself, whew, that was a slightly unnatural act. And it doesn't matter whether what got you to the Zone was a CEO slot, a book contract, a great teaching slot, or scaling a rock face.

I was still in my twenties when I set out to climb the Half Dome rock face in Yosemite National Park. For three nights, my partners and I slept in hammocks hanging over vertical drops as great as 1,500 feet. We scaled one big vertical crack system in the middle of crackling lightning. Finally, when we got within 150 feet of the top, my male partners raced on up and left me with all their backpacks to drag up along with my own. As I climbed over the rounded shoulder of the top and stood on solid ground for the first time in three days—with tears of exhaustion, relief, and pure fear streaming down my face—I felt two things: that I wouldn't trade the experience for anything I've ever done, and that I would kill myself before I tried anything like that again any time soon.

The question in the Zone isn't what you're going to hold on to so much as what you're going to give up next. Like so many transporting experiences, it's built on equal parts of exertion and sacrifice—of muscle tone, of time, of sleep, of hundreds of different kinds of attention big and small that in another time and world you would be sure to pay. A balanced life in the Zone is not only impossible but also self-destructive: Perfect balance equals perfect failure: It's that stark and simple. The only hope is that there will be enough to jettison around the edges that you won't have to give up the things that are truly central to your existence: your children, your spouse, what nourishes the spirit and soul. Sometimes, in truth, there just isn't.

> Imbalance is the name of the game. A completely rounded lifestyle just doesn't happen in the Zone. You can have perfect biceps later.

Necessary Losses

Former Secretary of Labor Robert Reich captures this dual sense of great happiness and potentially great loss—of being one creature inside the Zone and another outside it—almost perfectly in the introduction to his book *The Future of Success*:

"A few years ago," he writes of his time in the Clinton White House, "I had a job that consumed me. I wasn't addicted to it—'addiction' suggests an irrational attachment, slightly masochistic, compulsive. My problem was that I loved my job and couldn't get enough of it. Being a member of the President's cabinet was better than any other job I'd ever had. In the morning, I couldn't wait to get to the office. At night, I left it reluctantly. Even when I was at home, part of my mind remained at work.

"Not surprisingly, all other parts of my life shriveled into a dried raisin. I lost touch with my family, seeing little of my wife or my two sons. I lost contact with old friends. I even began to lose contact with myself—every aspect of myself other than what the job required."

The most simple loss lies at the heart of all the complicated consequences that flow from being in the Zone: time, sheer hours in a day, days in a week, sometimes even months in a year. In the Zone, there is never enough time; yet until you step outside and have a look, it's almost impossible to realize that. "This is not about business hours," Todd Wagner, the CEO and founder of Broadcast.com, told Bob Reich for his book. "It is about waking hours. You try to do as much as you can for as long as you can stay awake."

Once upon a time, as Reich notes, there was a reward for all this labor: You'd find a market niche, a product stability, and you could begin to coast a little, begin to win back the hours you had put in the bank. In the new calculus of global competition, shortened product cycles, and almost constant start-ups nibbling at every angle of your business, though, that point simply never comes as fully and completely as you expected. "I was naive," Alan Webber, the cofounder of Fast Company, told Reich. "I thought that once we had the magazine up and running, and hit our targets, we would relax. But now we have to work even harder to stay ahead of the pack." We Internet CEOs used to have a running joke among ourselves: The perfect job would be exactly 50 percent of the one we were doing—35 hours a week instead of 70.

With an eye toward reclaiming some of our lost hours, Nancy Evans and I took a week at the Canyon Ranch spa, the Arizona fitness resort, at the height of iVillage's rise. We had a new product to work on (nothing in the Zone is ever solely about leisure), but during dinner one night, we ended up going off task and making a list of everything we did in a week, in both our work and our home lives, from sealing deals to paying the babysitter and putting the kids to bed to our own sleep. I can't remember what Nancy's list added up to anymore—something huge—but my own came to 250 hours. Great, I thought, I've chronicled my life and I'm a master of the time universe. And then I realized that no matter how you did the math, a week added up to 168 hours, no more, no less. Where had those other 82 hours come from? Suddenly, I understood why I felt like I had been living in my Air Jordans for so long. Like every entrepreneur I've ever talked with about this, I literally had been running full tilt for nearly three years, trying to outrace the clock.

Nancy and I spent the next three evenings trucking extra food back to the room in our napkins (spa food cannot fuel the energy of the Zone) and trying to find a way to make the math of my life work. I was a single mom. I couldn't just cut out the personal hours. I couldn't cut the work hours either. I was CEO; I had a responsibility—fiduciary, moral, and in lots of other ways—to a whole network of people and institutions. In the end, I did what any reasonable person starting a company might do in my circumstances. I gave up sleep. And thus by pulling two all-nighters a week for a full year, I made my week fit into the 168 hours that the earth's rotation around the sun provided for it.

Eventually, even our insane industry would grow up a tad, and I could claim a little bit of sleep at least all seven nights of the week, but those "slow" years, as I've come to think of them, included taking the company public, doing a second offering in the public market, acquiring seven properties including our number two competitor, and weathering an average loss of 80 to 90 percent in the market capitalization of all companies in our sector in the very short and by now very infamous crash of April 2000.

No wonder that my six years at iVillage were enough for me: I lived maybe twice as many years in that time. And that really is the point of all this talk about the Zone. The Zone both elongates time and condenses experiences to their absolute essence. Yes, there is no balance, but there is in fact a glorious balance if you think of each chapter, each Zone, as part of the mosaic of your life's record.

Like Bob Reich, I'm convinced that the best jobs available to all of us in the years immediately ahead are going to have a "fire hydrant" (his words) quality to them. Turn them on and there's no modulation. Everything is full force all the time. Fresh off his Clinton White House experience—and teaching at Brandeis University as I write—Reich says the only real question is how much time you will spend in these exquisitely pleasing yet pressure-cooker positions. There's another, complementary way to approach all this, and that is to concentrate on the in-between periods, the gaps between the Zone, as much as we concentrate on the Zone itself.

In a life of serial reinvention, the "no-moments" count as much as the big moments. Use that time to find your own work infrastructure, your interests and unique abilities. Use it to listen to your inner voices, your regrets about the things not done, the people not seen to. Lie in your grave and listen to the eulogy and ask yourself whether you would miss or want what was said, but do the purely pleasurable things, too. Walk in the park, get perfect biceps (worth achieving several times in a lifetime), read more books, see more movies, brunch with more friends, do absolutely nothing with your kids as frequently as you can. Honor and explore and fully utilize this space between ecstasies; see to your quality of being; and you can emerge into each Zone, whatever it is you're doing, stronger than before and more ready to take advantage of every glorious moment.

The experience won't always be the same. Lives change. The way joy expresses itself to us changes. Age and experience temper all of us. "The younger I was, when I had all the energy in the world, it seemed sweeter," Bob Kerrey says of the Zone. "I had more energy. Life was beautiful. There weren't any bad guys. Over the years, you learn to deal with loss: the loss of a mom, of a dad, of innocence, in my case the loss of a limb. Now, being there just seems nicer. I feel more grateful today, more gratitude than I did when I was 25."

In my entrepreneurial chapter, no moment shone more brightly than when I first saw the iVillage symbol flicker across the ticker at Goldman Sachs. The other day, in my new chapter, I took my girls out to get a frog in a baggie and ended up with an aquarium, three colors of gravel, guppies,

> This, too, will pass. Nothing as red hot as the Zone can last forever, but if you are lucky, you might get to spend 35 years of your life in a succession of Zones that marry your changing dreams and reality.

crabs, turtles, a blue lobster, and crickets for live feedings. Through it all, I was as rapt as I had been two years earlier in the Goldman Sachs trading room—and just as impressed with the laws of eat or be eaten.

Here, finally, is the true beauty of it all: If our lives operate in approximately seven-year cycles, as seems to be the case with me and many of my friends, and if we can expect to spend maybe five of those seven years in the white-hot center of our desire, and if it's not unreasonable in this day and age to expect, say, seven such seven-year cycles in a productive adult life, then if you are a really, really lucky person, it's possible to spend thirty-five years in this kind of fantastic alignment of who you are, who you are becoming, and what the possibilities are in each moment of your existence. All of this, I hope, explains why so many of us who live this way, and who have suffered all the pains just described, love the rigors of the Zone and go to such pains to structure our lives so that we can return there time and again. First, though, you have to learn to leave it well.

CHAPTER EIGHT

Leaving Well

When things reach maturity,
they decay of themselves.

—Lao-Tze

*I*n my dad's day, leaving well pretty much meant turning 65. The ceremonies and ritual gifts varied according to rank and attainment, but basically, for most workers—and particularly white-collar workers—there was one exit, preordained. You knew when old age began and what you were walking into, and thanks to fixed-benefit pensions, you also knew what you were carrying into your golden years.

Today, pensions are portable, companies disappear or are merged overnight, and job cycles—along with product cycles—have become so accelerated that a cresting experience is almost as likely to signal an abrupt end as a prolonged success. Six months before she closed the door on ingredients.com for good, Katherine Legatos was raising money at a remarkable rate and gaining plaudits both within and without the industry for her new product line, purely in the Zone and then just as purely outside it. Ingredients was, and then it wasn't.

In the last six years alone, the average tenure of a professional job has shrunk from ten years to four. One in seven workers changes jobs every year, all through the ranks and in every industry. Nearly 120 CEOs stepped down in each month of 2000, only 25 percent of them from Internet-related companies. Cyclical booms and busts come and go, but these are the substantive trends that shape our new world.

In fact, exits occur all the time in the work world today, departures we often never see coming. Craig Cohon was one of the anointed at Coca-Cola, a walk-on-water civilian. Not only had he been offered the biggest promotion of his life, but he and his wife had just committed to their dream vacation home. Why not? He had another 20 years left in the company, Coke certainly wasn't going anywhere, and like Katherine at ingredients.com, Craig was living in the intersection of his dreams and reality. A month later, he in effect made himself disappear. One inspirational speech, three days of soul searching with his wife, one call to his boss at corporate HQ in Atlanta, and Craig was suddenly somewhere and something else. A generation ago, it would have seemed a sign almost of psychological instability. At the beginning of the new century, it seems an act completely in concert with both the imperatives of change and the enormous opportunities those imperatives afford us, so radically has the work world changed.

I had coffee not long ago in Washington, D.C., with a woman in her early thirties who had spent the last five years with a local think tank. She wanted to make a transition from working on public policy to either journalism or writing. "I just feel like that chapter of my life is over," she told me. "It's time to start a new chapter."

"Why do you use the word 'chapter'?" I asked her. We were sitting at a sidewalk café just below Dupont Circle on a beautiful spring morning, only a five-minute walk from the White House.

"It's just how I've come to think of it," she said. "I've done the policy-wonk thing. I don't want to do it again. But it's like the chapters of a book. The experience doesn't disappear. Everything else just builds on top of it."

The young know. Many of them are already living this way because they see the reality of the world as it is with fresh eyes.

Bill Bridges makes the argument that all jobs today are temporary: yours, mine, everyone's. As if to emphasize the point, Bill, one of the most commercially successful of all writers on these subjects, works out of a small office over a coffee shop, near the old hippie enclaves of California's Mill Valley. Even the most tradition-bound professions would seem to bear out Bill's belief in the almost total portability of the workplace. The lore of blue-chip independent schools is replete with tales of headmasters and headmistresses who stayed in office almost forever, shaping the lives of generations of students. John McPhee's book *The Headmaster* tells the story of one of the most famous of the breed — Frank Boyden, who led Deerfield Academy in Massachusetts for 66 years before stepping down in June 1968. Today, according to the National Association of Independent Schools, a private school headmaster or headmistress is likely to leave his or her post after only six years, and one in three doesn't last a full three years in the job.

At the peak of our affection for and involvement in our work, at the heart of the Zone, we need to ready ourselves emotionally to leave because the statistics above don't lie—our jobs and our commitment to it are both on loan—and because the difference between maximizing our contribution and staying too long is just as thin as the horizon. At the peak of our success, we also need to begin looking around for our successor. Otherwise, the job will own us. Our exits, in short, are as important as our entrances, and the more fully we give ourselves over to serial reinvention, the more true that is.

> When endings become a way of life, being prepared for departure is as important as being successful at the job itself.

Power Outages

Sometimes our departures announce themselves like a cannon shot. Robert Reich writes of the time he called home from his office at the Labor Department to tell his two sons that he wouldn't be home in time to say good night: "I'd already missed five bedtimes in a row. Sam, the younger of the two, said that was O.K., but asked me to wake him up whenever I got home. I explained that I'd be back so late that he would have gone to sleep long before; it was probably better if I saw him the next morning. But he insisted. I asked him why. He said he just wanted to know I was there, at home. To this day, I can't explain what happened to me at that moment. Yet I suddenly knew I had to leave my job."

More often the alarm clock, if it rings at all, is a collection of small clues, absences as much as presences. "I think every successful person sooner or later feels cut off by the demands of success from some inner treasure—something inside that could provide fulfillment and make a unique contribution to the world, if only we could get at it," John O'Neil writes in *The Paradox of Success*.

For Dan Lewis, the messages to leave—his deteriorating sense of belonging in investment banking, the bad boss, the feelings that he was being required to live up to a different psychological contract than the one he had signed on to— were complemented by ironic opportunity. He had been divorced not long before he pulled the plug. When he finally moved across the country after seven months in the desert, he was traveling light. But it was his fortieth birthday party, Dan told me, that really prepared him for the call that drove his stake in the ground.

"The birthday was a lightning rod opportunity to get my family and friends together and do an accounting of the personal relationships that I had developed in my first 40 years. Besides my family, I think the median time that I knew anybody at the party was 25 years. The youngest friend I had there had been a six-year friendship. I was truly struck by that, and I was proud of the longevity of those relationships. It helped me get comfortable with the fact that I didn't have to define myself by my work. There was more to me than that."

Dan Lewis was lucky. He saw what the inner treasure was for him; he was able to follow it across the country to happiness. Too often, we get blinded to our central desires by the external treasures that we can't take our eyes off. Time and again, Dan said, he has found himself trying to counsel people who would be him but can't because they refuse to look deep into themselves.

"I can't tell you how many investment bankers I've had in my office, asking me, 'How did you do this?' So many of them frankly have some big amount of money in mind, and they are always saying, 'Well, I need one more or two more or three more years until I get there and until I get this and that.' Yet they're paying the government 55 percent between city, state, and local taxes, and all the other things. It's very hard to make huge sums of money under those circumstances unless you have significant equity participation, and nobody's giving that up without a fight. So these guys are living in a world where they haven't put themselves in much of a position to win.

"They're always postponing. I ask them, 'When do you want to start living?' Some of them, it turns out, love investment banking. Good for them. They should stay in it for the rest of their lives. But so many of them are really just risk averse."

Of all those who have come to him for advice, Dan told me, maybe one in twenty, at best one in ten, is able to let go of the numbers in his head and pursue instead the dictates of his heart. It should be scary. In fact, it's just the way things are. A couple of years back, I asked my then boyfriend, a wonderful and highly successful guy, what his number was—how much money he would need to have on hand before he could quit the job he so clearly hated. He told me $1 billion. Go through the math with me, I urged him. Even with extraordinarily elegant standards, why does anyone need $1 billion? We never got through the process, or beyond it, but a year later

> High-water marks rarely are. Telling yourself you won't leave until you've reached some artificial number, however well meant, traps you in an expectations game that can be hell to escape.

he quit his job, finally convinced that he was using the number in his mind as a way to postpone indefinitely the rest of his life.

Lots of us have numbers, and they don't need to have so many zeros behind them. Maybe it's whatever will pay off the mortgage and give us the house free and clear, or enough to guarantee the kids can get through college. One horse-race fan I know has a truly exact number: $76,722. That's how much he figures he lost at the track before he hit upon his current system of handicapping. (The number, as he keeps noting, is open to periodic reevaluation.) I've had my own numbers. At one time I'd set a goal of having $5 million by the time I was 50. Then, when iVillage began to roar, I raised the bar to $50 million, and from there to $100 million. Thank God, the Internet bubble market crashed before I took the bar in my mind to my own $1 billion. I had no more need of it than my old boyfriend did, and pursuing it would have blinded me, as so many of Dan Lewis's associates have been blinded, to the transitions going on inside me, under my very nose.

No matter what your number is, you've got two problems: First, you may never get there, and second, if you do, you tend to raise the stakes. "I had watched our friends set these targets and then ratchet them up and up," Jeanette Cohon, Craig's wife, told me. "It's a line that moves with what you have. There's no way to declare victory. I decided to get off."

David Zelman calls all this an "artificial imposition on being." We won't step off the corporate merry-go-round until our assets reach $10 million. We won't give up the national desk until we've won a Pulitzer. What seemed impossible can suddenly seem impossibly close: After two years of back-breaking labor, the grant to expand our community outreach looks as though it finally will be approved next month. What seemed an impediment to happiness can suddenly become its imperative. We won't step down from the chair until we've cracked the Fortune 500. We won't leave the university presidency until the endowment tops $2 billion. We've all been there: "Won'ts" can be far louder than "wills." In my case, this took the form of telling myself I wouldn't leave the CEO slot at iVillage until I'd seen the company to profitability. As I was beginning to dream of escape, profitability was another 18 months away, Worse, while we were exactly on plan, my goal flew in the face of the onslaught of internal signals I was receiving after five and a half years on the job. The world is organic, David Zelman told me. Unless we march to the real drum that beats within us, creativity dries up. We become the slaves of false ambition, the beginning of death in life. He was right. For a moment at least I did just that.

Burn Out, Chill Out, and Déjà Vu All Over Again

Another scene that sticks with me from my last months at Time Warner: I'm attending a meeting on the company's database strategy when suddenly I have this overwhelming sensation that I've been dropped into the middle of the Bill Murray comedy, *Groundhog Day*. I knew with what seemed an absolute certainty that I

The Bill Murray rule: When your life seems like *Groundhog Day*, it's time to go.

had already attended this meeting, sat at this very spot around the table as these very people defended the very same positions, and what's more, that I'd done this time and again. Like Bill Murray, I couldn't figure out why the experience wasn't driving everybody else nuts.

Not long ago, I ran into the woman who had taken over my job at American Express in 1989 and was still doing it almost a dozen years later. Over the same time, I had been in two more industries, been through two more Zones, and been part of a large group of pioneers who collectively helped commercialize the Internet, and I'd left all that to write this book and start a new career as a teacher, speaker, and mentor. What was it like to deal with the budget process the twelfth time around, I wanted to ask her? But I didn't want to be rude, and besides, she may be able to uncover novelties in the work that I was unable to see.

We can burn out from repetition — "déjà vu all over again," as Yogi Berra once put it — or we can burn out from simply burning too bright. Even before we cross the 80-hour-week work threshold, a kind of tunnel vision tends to set in. Other parts of existence fall away, parts that would leaven our spirit and broaden our attention in other circumstances. Instead, we become focused on whatever is pulling us forward, often to the ultimate disbenefit of not just ourselves but the organizations we serve. "Hubris appears when observation fails," John O'Neil writes. "A race to the prize cuts off peripheral vision. It blinds us to changes in the marketplace, discontented employees, stirrings in ourselves. In time, the tunnel vision blossoms into tunnel lives, and the more so, the higher the position and the more naturally isolated it already is."

After I read his book, John and I got together to talk at his San Francisco office surrounded by woods in the Presidio. Silicon Valley was all of 20 minutes away. The Golden Gate Bridge was much closer, hidden from us by the thick growth of trees. John's space was built for contemplation and for getting beyond the usual taboos in talking about life at the top of the executive ladder.

"What happens to hyper-busy people?" John O'Neil asked rhetorically. "You and I know the answer. They can't have mentors. They can't sit down, put their feet up, and have a two-hour conversation in the middle of the day as we're doing. They can't do it. 'My schedule is this. I can't do it. I'm just so busy.' And so they get caught up in this bizarre game. This dance that they're in denies the very advice and very thinking they need.

"I once sat with my brother-in-law in a lovely old place on the Florida Keys called the Anglers Club. We sat there and he said, 'Look, we're sitting in the middle of one of the fanciest clubs in the world, and there are all these CEOs and chairs. They've all been here day after day after day. They'll be here tomorrow. And what do they talk about? They talk about golf and the stock market, maybe occasionally politics, but not too seriously. When did the lights go out?'

"And, you know, he was right. Their lights do just go out. It's not really burnout. Young people get burned out. They're like the lamps that just get too hot. I call this 'chill out' instead. I look around that room in the Anglers Club on the Keys and whom do I see? Chill outs. There's no fire to them. They're all about comportment, they're all about image, but there's no fire in the belly. There's no youth left. It's like premature aging."

In his book, John O'Neil suggests an 11-question personal survey that can help everyone, not just CEOs, short-circuit the "chill out" he has just described—questions such as "In what way is your work consistent with your self-image and what way inconsistent?" "What are you most afraid of?" And "How have your goals changed?" Just as important, John says, is to consistently expose yourself to what he calls "fresh learning": subjects, people, and situations that challenge and broaden your understandings instead of simply confirming and thus narrowing them. Often the message that it's time to leave arrives up a side street when we're exploring new territory, but unless you venture into that fresh terrain, you'll never receive it. Afternoons at the Anglers Club are about the past, not the future.

By way of contrast, a professor told me the story of a former chief financial officer for one of the pharmaceutical giants. He had retired at 65, expecting to golf his way through his summer and winter "communities." Two years later, bored beyond description, he started a company that leased space to infant biotechnology companies. Suddenly, he was a gray-haired eminence in a struggling industry. Far more important, he was revitalized physically, mentally, even spiritually. To pull his old peers into the same Zone he had fallen into, this man started a club for other retired high-ranking executives. The criterion for membership: You have to make an investment in a biotech start-up and agree to become a functional officer—someone with his sleeves rolled up, on the hook for making it happen, not sitting at the comfortable remove of the boardroom—of the company you invest in. That's having the gumption to take a work life seemingly at an end and plow it back into the earth so that others can grow where you have been.

Knowing Who You Are and Where You Fit

Just as people fit into organizations in different ways at different points in their lives, so organizations fit each of us differently as we travel through adulthood. It's an extraordinarily fluid person who can match up successfully within the same corporate structure at every rung of the ladder and at every niche along the way, and an extraordinarily fluid organization that can provide such matches.

I mentioned near the front of this book that Robert Levitan had left iVillage just on the verge of our IPO. He had been with Nancy and me from the beginning, cofounder and partner. Now, just as we were about to cash in our sweat equity for something closer to real money, Robert was gone. Where had the long knives come from? Who had tripped the trap door? The answer was simple: No one had. Robert walked out of iVillage on his own, for the best of reasons. During the first three years of the company, Robert had made contributions without which iVillage couldn't have survived. He was a tireless cheerleader for the cause. He had seemingly unlimited energy and a transforming optimism that allowed him to commit to the impossible and deliver on it as if it had been plausible all along. Just as important, Robert was completely flexible about his role. Whatever it was that needed doing, often by yesterday, Robert would take it on. For a startup, he was a virtual alchemist. As iVillage grew, though, it inevitably became a different company, first in degree and then in kind. We still needed energy and optimism, and Robert continued to provide both of them. But solo victories and cowboy forays became less important than specialized talent and structured responses.

In an ideal world, maybe, we would have found a way to weave Robert into a fabric of roles and responsibilities that fit our needs as well as his. He had, after all, been instrumental in creating us. In the real world we operated in, though, he started to uncouple from what the company had become. Other members of the management team became increasingly frustrated with him. At the same time, he began to chafe. Finally, in the fall of 1998, on almost the very eve of our IPO, Robert told me that he wanted to leave to colaunch another new start-up. I would have liked for all three of us to have stood together in the Goldman Sachs trading room at the moment the company we had struggled to build first went public, but I knew in my bones that Robert's contribution to iVillage had peaked, and I knew that he knew it. What Robert did was, in fact, noble. He recognized—not without pain—that the company had moved past the point where his contributions and his satisfaction were optimal.

What Robert needed was another blank page, another small team of underdogs fighting for their lives with the odds stacked desperately against them, depending on Robert Levitan to do the impossible for them, and that's just what he got with Flooz, a wonderful company that Robert has helped build into a leader in the online gift-certificate business. In the end, Robert gave us all a great lesson in how to leave well. He understood himself, and because he did, he was able to give up what might have made him rich for what will probably make him both happy and rich.

Robert's early departure from the company had one ironic consequence: He was able to cash out his stock at around $100 a share, something the rest of us didn't get to do. But happy, not rich, is the point here. The push toward a great departure can have an epic quality to it. Money, fame, status — elements of Maslow's famous hierarchy of needs — drive almost all of us forward to a greater or lesser extent, but as generations of the truly rich have discovered, those same impetuses often evaporate once you get to the top. In the Zone, money can have an intoxicating flavor; outside, it quickly becomes empty calories. In *The Gospel of Wealth*, published in 1889, Andrew Carnegie argued that the first half of a rich man's life should be devoted to making money and the second half to giving it away for the benefit of the public. Carnegie followed his own advice after J. P. Morgan bought out his steel interests for $240 million, funding among other things a library system that helped to educate generations of city dwellers in the United States and his native Great Britain. At John D. Rockefeller's prime in the 1910s, when his worth climbed to nearly a billion dollars and he was arguably the world's most reviled man, he was giving money away as fast as he could make it in an attempt to balance his spiritual account with his temporal one.

Like many people who lived through the heady days of dot-coms, I became suddenly wealthy beyond my wildest expectations — and then, just as suddenly, not so wealthy. My own experience of being worth in excess of $100 million, if only on paper and only for a few months, permanently altered my motivation. Suddenly, being a Master of the Universe seemed infinitely less important than giving away whatever I could and helping to make the world a better place. Time and again when I talk to people who have been through the same experience — people whose worth shot up into the nine and ten and eleven figures during the market run-up of the late 1990s–I hear the same story: They went to bed rich, and they woke up in the morning feeling a compelling need to accomplish something beyond themselves, to make something other than money. They, too, had stepped outside of the Zone. They had come uncoupled from the mother ship, as surely as Robert Levitan did, as surely as I eventually did. My own sense is that the sum total of all these uncouplings is going to make philanthropy one of the great growth "industries" of the next two decades. You can only spend so much.

More often what drives us toward the exit door are matters so trivial we'd be hard-pressed to tell our spouses or friends about them. I remember so well the first day at iVillage of a woman who had come to us from Morgan Stanley, one of the oldest of the establishment investment banks. I was making small talk with her when I happened to notice that she was wearing sandals and a lovely blue polish on her toenails that I instantly envied. When I told her so, she responded with great joy, "I knew this was a great choice! At Morgan Stanley, I had to hide my toenail polish." Trivial? Sure, but there was a hidden message in those displayed toenails, one deep and resonant enough to detach her from one of the world's great banking houses and land her in a helter-skelter Internet start-up where we had far more things to worry about than whose toes showed what.

In 1993, I was locked in a battle with the real estate group at Time Warner over whether I could have a dark-green couch instead of a dark-blue one. Dark green happened to suit me better. If nothing else, it would satisfy my rising desire for a measure of self-expression. Dark blue, on the other hand, was standard issue for the rung and space I had ascended to, and at Time in those days, standard issue had almost religious significance. The battle was inching forward at a water-torture-like pace when one day I walked into designer Diane von Furstenberg's office, took a look at her pink walls and leopard-skin rugs, and knew with a certainty that my days of standard issue were over. Until that moment, I never realized how much of my new rising self I was having to park outside the door when I showed up for work.

Success can be a prison, John O'Neil writes, and the greater the success, the thicker the walls. Powerful CEOs get trapped inside their own past triumphs and everyone else's expectations of more of the same. "I just want to sweep everything off my desk," one highly successful retail executive told John. "I don't want to deal with my past anymore. I want to start freshly. I want that sense of not knowing and mastering and succeeding at something for the first time. It's like wanting to fall in love passionately again. Sometimes when I go to bed, I think: I don't want to wake up in this bed, in this city again. Could I wake up in a tent and hear lions roaring outside? Could I wake up on another planet?"

Nothing stays the same. Even great success can morph into something far removed from what we wanted in the first place, and when that happens, it can bury us alive.

That's uncoupling, too. When our dreams are one place and we're another, not moving toward them, we're always less than whole. But getting from one to the other takes acts of courage that not all of us are capable of, at least in giant leaps. One good friend left his job in stages: a leave of absence here, a cutback in hours there, all the while both divorcing himself emotionally from people he had spent 11 years working with side by side and trying out a new person who needed less corporate support and more individual space to operate in.

Michelle Smith, the financial adviser to people in transition, had one client who marshaled her resources for five years before pulling the plug on her old life. The reward has been an extraordinary wide window for planning her next chapter.

Don Marrs uncoupled himself from Leo Burnett in sequence: quitting his high executive position at the corporate headquarters, moving out to Los Angeles for the far less prestigious position of making commercials, each step a kind of evolutionary parole from the jail he found himself living in but none of them definitive enough to accomplish the break he so desired until finally he got an ultimatum: Come back to Chicago and take up his old job or be fired. "I was like a cub who got scared and stopped at the icy edge of the stream," Don writes. "What I needed was a swift swat on the behind."

Part of the challenge of management in this new world is to recognize those decoupling moments in our colleagues and underlings, and to accept them for what they are: Natural progressions in a world ruled by change, not stasis; by reinvention, not repetition. Equally, part of the challenge of self-management also is to recognize these moments in ourselves, the court of last resort where work and happiness are concerned.

In my American Express days, I ran a group that was doing a great job and having lots of fun. It was, I honestly believed, the work I was meant to do at the place I was meant to do it, and I had every intention of doing it for years. Then one day a senior vice president in charge of the group next to mine on the floor where we worked came to tell me that he had asked that we be moved to another location because our laughter was distracting his team. At that instant, I had a moment of total clarity. For me, humor was one of the most important survival skills in the work world as well as a spiritual link to my tribal days in the mountains. It would be two more years before I finally left the company—I can have gut-check problems, too—but at that moment the pod that is me took off from the mother ship that was American Express and never ever came back.

I was thrilled when we were able to attract Betty Hudson to iVillage. Betty had done public relations for Reader's Digest Association and NBC, and was one of the most admired executives in New York City. She did a great job for us, too, but one day she announced that her husband was moving to Washington, D.C., in response to a great opportunity at the National Geographic Society, and that she would be going with him. Stay, I begged her, at any cost—you name the terms. And then I saw the light: Betty had come to her own turn in the road. Her story line was changing, in a world where change was natural, not the exception. All I could do was stop, note the loss, and wish her the best of luck. Six months later, over lunch, Betty told me about the work trip she and her husband had just returned from—a week in Machu Picchu with their children. The two of them work at the same company now, an easy 10-minute commute from their new home. It's hard to argue that she should have stayed put.

Swats on the behind, wake-up calls, gut checks, label them what you will. They are all part of our internal tom-tom system, the thumps-thumps and semaphores and smoke signals that tell us both when it's time to leave and where our next success lies. As with so much else we're concerned with here, the trick is to be quiet enough in the din of our days and nights to hear them, and to let others hear theirs. There's more to it than that, though.

Exits Have a Life of Their Own

Much of this book is a distillation of lessons painfully learned, by me and by others. One of the most painful of those lessons is this: Once we hear the voices telling us it's time to go, we have to honor them. To truly leave well, we need to have faith that our instincts are speaking the truth to us, and we can't let anyone dissuade us from our new path, no matter how well-meaning they might be. In the Zone, we create force fields around us, enormous ambient energy. Once we decouple ourselves from the Zone, our energy becomes decoupled, too. Unless we get out of its way and get ourselves out of the way of the organization we have served, the energy that has sustained us for so long can engulf us instead, and even destroy some of the best of what we have created. Beware of what you wish for, the old saying goes, and with cause: Wishes really can move mountains—I know that now. The trouble is, we're never entirely certain which way the mountain will go.

At the very moment when I was standing in a living room in Greenwich, Connecticut, with Nancy Evans, trying to help her find the light at the end of her own tunnel, all the subplots of my life converged. The time had come for me to leave iVillage. After five unbelievable years building the company, I had begun suddenly to resent the trade-offs I had been forced to make between my life and my work. My family had expanded when Ellie, my toddler from Hungary, had joined Michaela, and they both wanted more of me. For half a decade I had been the public face of a very public company, 24 hours a day, 7 days a week, 365 days a year. Where was the private woman inside that public face, I wondered, and when would I get to represent her?

I also resented the ambivalence about femininity and leadership that I finally had been forced to admit was real. When the irate mail began to pour in about a fur-trimmed hat I happened to be wearing when I was interviewed outdoors during a snowstorm at the 1999 Davos forum, something snapped in me. In the Zone, all of this stuff washes over you. Screw 'em, you think. I'm on a roll, in the absolute conjunction of my dreams and my reality. (As Marie Antoinette put it, more eloquently, "Let them eat cake.") Out of the Zone, as just mentioned, the energy remains, but now it begins to convert to fury. It was just a hat, for God's sake. Because I was slipping outside the iVillage Zone, I was also beginning to feel the many subtle pressures to bury the feminine side of my personality and all its trappings in order to fit the required look and feel of a public company CEO. Before, I had been willing to do what was necessary. Now, I was growing my hair and buying brocade and lace.

Without realizing it, I had drawn my own line in the sand. No doubt, too, I was just plain tired. I'd been trying for five years to be the best CEO I could be of a fast-growing, now public company that was occupying a significant slot in the Internet space where for years smart people—people I otherwise respected and sometimes even deferred to—said women would never congregate. (As I write, women make up half of the estimated Internet population of 100 million users.) I'd been trying also to be the best mommy I could be, and now my newest child, it turned out, needed an enormous amount of special treatment and attention. I remember every nuance of a meeting I sat through with the headmistress of the pre-school Ellie was then attending. What did she need, I kept asking? What could we give her? CEOs command resources.

We solve problems. We are operational people, action-oriented. What Ellie really needed, of course, was more of me—the one thing, by then, I felt I had no more left to give.

For one bright shining moment as I stood in that Greenwich living room, the course of action before me shone bright as a diamond. I really believe that leadership and building a company are like a relay race. The first leg belongs to the jack rabbits—people who can burst out of the starting blocks. Next come the CEOs who keep the momentum going, first in the evolution to a successful operating company, then in the big scaling push that follows. Finally there's the closer, the one who breaks the tape and institutionalizes the victory. Many of the people I had most admired in business had run the race just that way—passed the baton on at just the moment when their own contribution had maximized. I had listened in horror not long before as a colleague of mine in the Internet space said he hoped to die in his job. That just wasn't me, and it would never be. What's more, the company was beginning to experience the kind of stresses that I knew indicated we were in transit from one stage to another. Clearly, I thought, it's time for me to move on.

My first step was to call the board members I most trusted and tell them it was time to think seriously about succession. No way, they in essence told me. It was too soon. Everything was fine. I was at a bump in the road, but I'd get over it. (I happened to reach one of them on the ski slopes, which might have modulated his sense of urgency.) To be honest, I was flattered by their responses. Who doesn't like to hear she's indispensable? There were mitigating circumstances, too: The person we had had in mind all along to replace me was having increasing difficulties. Not only could she not step up in this time frame, but she would soon take herself out the door, turning what had been seen as a stately succession into a mad scramble. At the bottom line, though, I let myself override my own instincts, and for the next six months there was hell to pay.

Like untold others before me, I fell into the "won't" trap: I won't quit until the stock price is back up. Instead of letting myself be guided by the loud voices deep within that were all saying "Go, go, go," I made myself the slave of a number I couldn't begin to control. Suddenly, my life's clock wasn't mine at all any more. As the Nasdaq dropped like a rock in my final six months as iVillage's CEO, our stock tumbled with it. Meanwhile, I was losing the will required to lead. Ultimately, I was able to hand over the CEO reins roughly on schedule to an able person who was more right, and far more rested, for the job after a two-year hiatus since his own last chapter change. And I did learn a lesson that I intend to take with me for the rest of my life: I will never, ever override my instincts again. Whether we're crazy or sane, those inner voices speak to us for a reason.

Energy Leaks and Lessons

"When I meet people who have had a great triumph, I tell them I hope it hasn't hurt them too much," Carl Jung once commented. In fact, the record books are full of examples of just what Jung was referring to: great inventors who never got beyond their first great invention, entrepreneurs who could never escape their first great idea, Pulitzer Prize winners who kept on writing the same story or book long after it had garnered them the award that drove them on in the first place.

Great success is often the after-image of great output. Our reputation continues to climb, honors and press clippings arrive with ever-great regularity, long after the energy that brought us to our point of maximum output has begun to leak away. That's human nature: We tend to celebrate excellence in its aftermath because it's only after its optimal moment has passed that we really notice the quality. It's human nature, too, to want to stay on after our own optimal moments have passed, to bask in the warm glow of our triumphs, but doing so always traps us in yesterday instead of moving us toward tomorrow.

In his chapter entitled "Anticipating Entropy" (*entropy* is the tendency of energy to dissipate), John O'Neil cites the example of Dr. Jonas Salk. Nearly five decades ago, Salk solved the riddle of polio by creating a vaccine from live cells of the virus, and in so doing he freed a whole generation from the specter of atrophied limbs and those frightening and cumbersome life-support machines known as iron lungs. Before the injectable Salk vaccine, and soon afterward the oral Sabin vaccine, America had been swept by periodic panics of almost horror-movie intensity—the summer of 1954, the year before the vaccine was widely available, had seen an especially bad epidemic of polio. Afterward, the disease simply seemed to disappear. Salk was hailed as a miracle worker, further endearing himself to the public by refusing to patent the vaccine. If ever anyone deserved to rest and receive the gratitude of a grateful nation, it was Jonas Salk. Instead, Salk created the theory known as the "Epic B curve" (see Epic A/Epic B and Trial and Error on page 202), and he followed his own theorizing into a lifetime of serial scientific reinvention that, up until his death in 1995, kept him searching for a vaccine against AIDS.

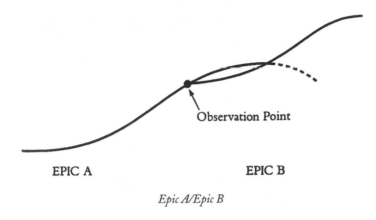

Observation Point

EPIC A   EPIC B

Epic A/Epic B

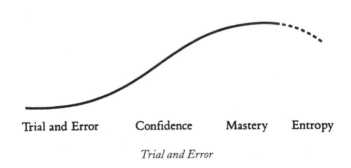

Trial and Error   Confidence   Mastery   Entropy

Trial and Error

Boiled down to its simplest elements, Salk's Epic B curve holds that knowledge grows rapidly around new paradigms and other insights until it reaches the top of a curve where entropy sets in and begins to pull the curve downward again. Beyond what has come to be known as the "observation point"—the point where learning starts to slow—the curve will continue to rise on the strength of its past momentum, but it becomes inefficient for any organism to spend more time there because the energy now being dissipated will always win out in the end. Instead, Salk argued—an argument he devoted his career to—it's at the observation point, while the trajectory is still upward, where you begin to need to look around for another paradigm or insight (or mission or company) to attach yourself to: the Epic B that leads to Epic C that leads to Epic D and so on.

"To imagine this," John O'Neil advises, "you might think of a surfer who senses the dynamic of the wave beneath him, and compare the observation point to the instant when he knows it is time to abandon the sinking or breaking wave and catch a new one that is building."

Another way to look at it—also suggested by John O'Neil—is to think of extreme mountain climbing. Sometimes expeditions can become so focused on the upward trajectory, on reaching the summit, that they neglect what in retrospect are obvious signs that the moment of maximum performance and optimal conditions has passed them by. Jon Krakauer's *Into Thin Air* is, in fact, a haunting and riveting example of just that: an Epic B curve that climbed straight past its observation point to the 29,028-foot crest of Mount Everest only to find itself so exhausted of energy and in such dire conditions that five of those scaling the mountain that day, including two of the most experienced expedition leaders in the world, would not survive.

You also might just consult your own professional life and the lives of those you've come to know well in your tour through the work world. Going past the observation point is easy, even if you're not oxygen-starved and snow-blinded as Krakauer's Everest team was. Pride intervenes, and the executive equivalent of the divine right of kings. You feel you've earned your place at the top. When you climb high enough up the curve, the position defines who you are, to the world and often to yourself. Getting off it can even seem counter-intuitive. Why work so hard only to leave? And yet once you pass the observation point, energy dissipation is exceeding energy generation. Something's got to go, and soon, and if you're going to leave well, if you're going to make a successful launch into the next chapter, the next wave, the next edition of yourself, that something really needs to be you. "Those who make the most graceful transitions," John O'Neil writes, "are those who know where they are, anticipate change, and prepare early."

What are the lessons in all this for leaving well? People can draw their own, but as I thought about all the reading I had done, the people I had talked with, the good and bad exits I had seen, and ones of both sorts I had lived through myself, five general principles suggested themselves:

Give up on trying to end at the top. Everyone wants to go out on a high note. I did at iVillage, and I got trapped by the share-price number that I thought would validate my exit. It's the rare person who, like Ted Williams, can crack a home run the last time at the plate and walk away from the game for good. More often, we stumble forward long after the spring has gone out of our legs. A good friend of mine, a very successful trader, returned 500 to 1 in his first fund. The trouble is, he continued trying to replicate that magical first moment while his returns got slimmer and slimmer—finally going negative—and his happiness quotient sank toward zero.

Finally, he got the message: Life is finite, and he was never going to get the years back he sank into a job that had long ago ceased to satisfy him. I happened to be around the day he closed the fund for good: It was like a boulder had been lifted off his shoulders. A life worth living isn't a single upward-tending thread; it's a tapestry woven of dozens upon dozens of experiences.

Get out while the getting is good. Heed your inner voices. Trust your instincts. And hang around as briefly as you can after you've made the decision to close a chapter. Remember Jonas Salk's Epic B curve: The energy is leaking out; what's left is likely to turn on you because you're putting it to false uses. Make a short list of what remains to be done in order to complete your contribution to the organization; then scratch out everything on the list over which you don't have direct control. I was intent on staying on at iVillage long enough to see our stock rebound because I thought a strong share price would be the final corollary proof to our strong leadership position in a lucrative market segment and results delivered consistently above the Street's expectations. Good enough, but neither I nor Alan Greenspan had any real control over what the market ultimately did. I can see now that I was on a fool's mission.

Don't just stomp out. Of all the exit strategies I've talked about with the people who inform this book, this is the only one that doesn't work virtually 100 percent of the time. Saying "Screw you, I'm outta here" feels good for about five minutes. After that, the taste turns sour fast and reality comes scuttling in. A literary agent I've known for years who tried the "screw-you" exit reports that it increased by months the duration and difficulty of his transition, while buying him a very fleeting satisfaction. Chris Ogden was so convinced that the world of commercial cable held no further meaning for him and so fed up with the person he had become that he walked in and quit on the spot. All of that was fine for high drama, but suddenly, a person who had defined himself by money and status had neither and no clear idea of what he wanted to become, either. Quitting on the drop of a dime can be a kind of bracing shock therapy, but laying a little groundwork for where you're going next before you walk out the door makes for more graceful exits and entrances.

"Screw-you" exits tend to screw only one person: you. Even when you know in a flash that it's time to leave, bide your time. The knowledge that the end has come will bring it to pass, and in the right way.

Have some muscle in reserve to help get your fingers unwrapped from the ledge. The last moments of any chapter have a built-in poignancy that is all the greater when you have lived in the heart of your dreams and desires. Yes, you feel the restlessness. Yes, you hear a calling. Yes, you're out of gas and you know it. It's time to go. If you need one, you've got a successor in place, ready to step into your shoes. Intellectually, that's swell. Emotionally, those last five minutes can be just sheer hell. The number you set in your mind that the company had to reach before you departed was too low— $1 billion in sales is just down the road! Why didn't I realize that we would hit our 10 millionth customer next month? At last, I've got the volunteers I need to truly get the job done! You walk down the hall and feel a deep nostalgia for a place and a life that the other side of your brain knows is the past, not your present or future. Or you walk down the same hall and just know that the person about to step into your office is itching to undo some of the things you count among your dearest accomplishments. The Beatles had it right: Let it be.

John O'Neil told me a story about a client who made careful plans to move from CEO of his company to chairman of the board, a job with fewer responsibilities and a lot less pressure. He was just about to execute those plans when he panicked, and John had to be called in to pry his fingers from the window ledge. I'd been there myself. I was as eager as anyone could be to end my chapter as CEO of iVillage after more than five and a half years. Night after night I dreamed of the green grass that waited on the other side and of the fun I would have there. Yet in the month the transition was scheduled to happen, I absolutely freaked out. Finally, a cadre of good friends helped me let go. Like a reluctant parasailor standing on the beach waiting for the speed boat to take off, life without the sand under you seems insupportable—until you're in the air and weightless, and never want this new sensation to end.

Don't expect a perfect bow on your exit. It's not just your own ecosystem that gets torn apart when you leave a chapter. You've ripped something out of the ecosystem you've left behind, too, and the feelings and tensions on both sides take time to heal. A friend was telling me the other day about a luncheon that had been thrown for him at a wonderful Spanish restaurant in downtown Washington, D.C. A month earlier, he had finally severed his ties to the law firm he had been with for more than two decades, a place he said he had absolutely loved until almost the exact moment when he absolutely loathed it and his life there. Two months later he had told his fellow partners he was leaving. Now they were throwing this bash for him, in a private dining room, except two of the partners ostentatiously hadn't shown. One had found a thin reason to take the morning shuttle to Boston. The other had an out-of-town client to entertain. Why, my friend had asked me? After all those years? Well, I asked, how had you behaved toward them recently? Miserably, he answered, but I was miserable! And with that he understood.

> It's the timing that matters, not the applause. The complicated dynamics of endings don't lend themselves easily to curtain calls.

We come uncoupled. The Zone we are headed for isn't the one they're still living in. The center doesn't hold. We miss the affection for the person we once were even as we move toward something else.

Another friend, a successful president of a public company, was fired when a new CEO took over. How long did it take him to get over the experience, I asked? "Oh," he answered, "on one level only 24 hours, on another level six to nine months, and on another six years." The figure was exact because he remembered the exact moment: He'd run into the CEO at an event a half dozen years after he had been sacked and congratulated his executioner on his success. Later that day, when the CEO was giving a presentation, he went out of his way to say how important my friend had been to the company's growth. Case closed, and ecosystem restored. But not easily. And not fast.

Craig Cohon left Coca-Cola of his own volition, but he almost inevitably carried some unfinished business with him. He had put in almost 20 years of his life with the company. Now that he stepped outside of it, he could see how at odds his corporate life had been with his deeper ambitions. A year passed before he could go back to his old CEO and ask him to commit the company to an investment in Global Legacy. Yes, the CEO said, and the two Zones were joined.

I was recently at a conference with iVillage's former chief financial officer. He'd left the company six months earlier, fried by living on Internet time after a long career in a very slow-moving, traditional company. He spoke and left to catch a plane before I arrived so I had to ask the audience what he had said. The answer both shocked and pleased me: Working for iVillage, he had told the gathering, had been the most valuable experience of his professional life because it was there that he learned what he was able to do. It wasn't something he could have felt or said a year earlier.

My stint working for Barry Diller offered much the same exquisite pleasure-pain experience. Undoubtedly, Q2 was the toughest year and a half of my working life. I'm not alone among the alums of Diller Academy in swearing to that; many of them literally take a few years off to recover from the ride. But whenever I'm asked what my most valuable experience of working with a boss has been, I always say much the same thing my old CFO said: Being with Barry taught me what I had inside: vision, determination, and the capacity to inspire others to build a dream.

With patience, our exits work themselves out. Done right, they also lead us to grand entrances. The secret is always to remember that we're not alone in these journeys and never to forget that finally we have to follow a road map that exists for us alone.

CHAPTER NINE

The New Social Contract

He grows accustomed only to change, and ends by
regarding it as the natural state of man.
He feels the need of it, more, he loves it;
for the instability, instead of meaning disaster
to him, seems to give birth only to
miracles all about him.

—Alexis de Tocqueville

Sam and Susan Gardiner met and married more than a dozen years ago when they were both working for one of the high-tech glamour companies. From there, they moved on to become part of a small team of senior executives at a hot publicly held company that became a darling of Wall Street. Sam particularly looked to be on the A track toward the presidency until, after a brief but intense period of mounting personal and professional tensions, he was fired and Susan was made president instead.

This was Sam's fourth chapter, a language he and I know now, but didn't know when he was going through the worst of this. He had had successful careers in government, academia, and elsewhere in the corporate world. Now, he faced trying to launch a fifth chapter, but he had made no preparations for his departure, and he had no idea where he was headed next or when he would get there. Rudderless, depressed, and with no map to guide him, Sam spent 18 of the most difficult months of his life. Susan, meanwhile, had gone into her own Zone, living fully in the office she had ascended to and paying less and less attention to her personal life at a time when Sam's personal life mattered more to him than it ever had before.

In the normal course of events, all of this should have been an almost sure formula for divorce and bitter memories, and in truth, it nearly was. Not only had Sam and Susan come uncoupled from one another; their lives were moving to different rhythms and reward structures. Then, almost as suddenly as Sam had been let go, a new CEO was named to lead the company where Susan remained, and his first act in office was to fire Susan. Happily for Susan—for them both, really—she already had a Navigator in place, someone who was just coming out of the other end of that sense of falling that she was just headed into.

In time, two life rhythms that had drifted badly out of synch began to find a kind of harmony again. With Sam's help, Susan was back on her feet in less than six months, with a new road map in hand for where her life was headed next. Within a few years of being axed as president, she was leading a start-up that became highly successful. With his personal life finally in calm waters, Sam found his next calling, too: a powerful desire to put his varied experience in business, academia, and government to work for good causes. Today, he serves on numerous nonprofit boards, a portfolio that means far more to him in this new Zone than any portfolio of stocks and mutual funds.

When I talked with Sam and Susan, they both mentioned their new, hard-won respect for the power of change in individual lives to rip a marriage apart. Both of them are aware that it was mostly serendipity that saved their relationship. Had Susan not been passed over for the chairmanship of her old company, and been fired in the aftermath, it seems certain that the deep detachment that had settled into their personal lives would have made itself permanent. They were too close to the abyss already. Sam also said that he felt that the best defense against what he and Susan had gone through was simply to have an understanding of the process itself, an atlas of sorts that would help each of the partners better track their own and their mate's way through these undulating curves of Zones and interregnums.

"The worst part," Sam told me, "was not just my own sense of having been cut adrift but my complete inability to understand where Susan was and why she couldn't be with me, where I needed her, when I needed her. Fundamentally, I just felt alone, abandoned by the woman I loved at the worst possible time."

I think, in fact, that Sam and Susan have been unwilling pioneers in the formation of a new social contract—a compact between would-be life partners that is coming piecemeal into existence in large part because we finally have the language to understand and talk about what the two of them went through and what thousands upon thousands of other couples are going through even as I write.

Marry for all the chapters in your life, not just one. If you choose someone solely for what he or she is at the moment, you're going to experience disappointment rather than adventure.

Yes, people will still marry doctors and investment bankers and lawyers and be doctors' and bankers' and lawyers' spouses for the rest of their lives, but this is no longer a world where what delivers and conveys status will hold constant for most of us. Unless we can form arrangements that have as much built-in fluidity as the work lives we lead, the ambient change imperatives of our times will overwhelm relationships as thoroughly and completely as they have overwhelmed businesses. If we can form that new social contract, though — if we can learn to make our marriages and our families breathe in harmony with not just the chapters of our lives but the spaces in between them — I also firmly believe that it will open lives and relationships to enormous possibilities.

The New Face of Marriage

Sam and Susan went through hell to get to a higher level in their relationship. Jeanette and Craig Cohon show that, with luck and preparation and with anticipation of the lacerating effects that radical change can let loose in the confined space of a marriage, such knowledge doesn't have to be so painfully won.

In its broad details, Craig and Jeanette's story is not all that different from Sam and Susan's. Zones were changing. Stress fractures were showing all over the place. Here, however, is what makes the two stories different: At the same time he asked Coke to provide him with personal coaches, Craig insisted the company provide personal coaches for Jeanette as well. If he was going on a journey, as he clearly sensed might be happening, Jeanette was going to need to go on a journey, too, if their relationship was going to survive. And, in fact, that is just what happened.

After days upon days of intense guided self-exploration, Jeanette found a deep and deeply repressed longing to become a doctor. As a career aspiration, it made no rational sense whatsoever: She was 30 and pregnant with her first child, and she was in the midst of building her own successful career doing international development deals for a growing roster of media and tech companies. She and Craig had also only recently finished building a vacation home in her native Sweden that was meant to be a sheltering port in their whirlwind lives. What sane person would even consider medical school under such conditions? The answer, Jeanette found, was herself. She had already sent in her applications to med school when Craig heard Bill Clinton's speech at Davos. It was three o'clock on the morning after the speech when Craig turned to Jeanette in bed and said, "Are you with me?" Immediately and instinctively, Jeanette told me, she said, "Go for it!" And thus what had already promised to be a significant alteration of lifestyle—one income instead of two, a full-time student as well as a part-time mother—became a radical life retooling instead.

"Craig married me thinking that I was a businessperson who would then give it up to be a mom," Jeanette told me. "Now, all of a sudden we had children, and I was facing all these years of medical school. I'd be going 24/7, and I wouldn't be able to support him as he was getting Global Legacy started. It was tough for him. It took him some time to accept. But I didn't want to live with buried dreams for myself or for Craig."

Most of us don't get two coaches per family. Almost all of us, though, have resources we can exploit in similar situations: Navigators, an inner circle of friends, books. The important thing, really, isn't the professional level of help available to us as much as it is the vocabulary for discussion. Without the words, we have no conversation. Without the conversation, we're stuck.

Elizabeth Kubler-Ross didn't discover anything new when she laid out her famous five stages of grief. Humans had been going through all five stages since we first rose up out of the primal muck and began to feel emotions for one another. Kubler-Ross simply put into words a universal and species-wide process. But what a difference it made to have the words. Before, the anger that arrives at moments of intense sorrow like some hideously unwanted guest had always seemed at best deeply embarrassing, at worst a mark of a crippled character. Now, it was all part of a process that led, finally, to acceptance of loss. As the guilt disappeared, the discussion grew, and as the discussion grew, lives were bettered and consciences repaired. Words make a difference.

My own marriage didn't survive a decoupling much like that which Sam and Susan went through. My husband and I had met when we were both working for the National Outdoor Leadership School. Our relationship had been forged out of the shared experiences of designing and leading courses through the mountains. Technical climbs, back-country rescues, and the intense camaraderie of tribal living in open land were our common and extraordinarily intense bonds, the daily stuff of the Zone we shared. David and I both thought, I believe, that we had laid the foundation for a lifetime's relationship, but we didn't know then how Zones change and powerful forces intervene in the best-laid plans. When I followed my intense longing to attend Harvard Business School and join the corporate world, my husband came along to support me. He had his own goals beyond the mountains, and Harvard's John F. Kennedy School of Government helped point him toward them. The experience enriched him, to be sure, but it didn't fundamentally change his course. He was older, less inclined to radical alteration of his own Zone. Not me. I was younger. I'd seen less of the world. Harvard Business School showed me a canvas for leadership that I wanted to paint on. In the end, he went back to the mountains, and I stayed on the East Coast. Everything seemed so black and white, so all or nothing.

Was our split foreordained? Then, I might have said yes. Now, I don't think so. Although David and I were both smart and willing, we had no language available to us to talk about this divergence in our paths, and without the words we had almost no chance of arriving at a creative accommodation for our new and separate chapters.

Learn to live with asymmetry. The diverging paths of reinvention can destroy a relationship, or they can make it stronger.

Numerous studies point to the rising divorce rate as a leading indicator of the dislocation that has swept across American society over the last three decades. I'm not convinced. I think it may be a trailing indicator, the aftermath of lives and relationships already caught in these rising whirlpools of change and uncertain how to get out of them. To this day, 15 years later, I still believe that David and I could have made our marriage endure if we had shared a view of life as a collection of chapters. What we lacked wasn't just the words; it was the sense of fluidity the words can teach us.

Sharing the Status, and the Kids

My friend Sam went from a series of lucrative executive positions to a life on nonprofit boards. Craig Cohon gave up a chance to ultimately lead one of the great global corporations so that he could create a foundation to give away global corporate wealth. Another friend, Paul Lapides, stepped down as CEO of the company he had founded to take a university post teaching organizational behavior. As a single father, Paul was determined to spend more time with his kids: Teaching gave him that freedom of time.

Have they all fallen off the status train? Yes, absolutely, if status is defined by such markers as money, but I don't think money is going to be anywhere near as reliable a scoring system as it has been for much of human history. My sense is that money will be no more important than the time that money is supposed to buy. People will be judged as successes or failures on their totality—not just on the money-accumulation and power-accumulation chapters they have lived through, but on the chapters devoted to family and service and on how well they've gotten through bad times and on much else. What people are able to give up as they move through the reinventions of their lives will be as important as what they are able to keep. Fluidity will be a more important benchmark than cash.

Ironically, I think we already have a great example of this to point to, someone I've mentioned earlier. Taken part by part, Michael Milken's life is replete with flaws and down notes; taken collectively, it's almost a symphony, full of light and dark passages. And like any symphony, it can't be judged a success or failure solely on the strength of its overture or intermezzo or coda. You've got to sit through it from beginning to end to hear it all, and if you do that in Milken's case, you can't help, I think, but be awestruck by the range of expression—good and bad, up and down—possible within a single human life.

Upward mobility implies a simple linear progression: More follows more. In the rising world I envision, lives will be lived more as wave functions, and the success or failure of each wave will be measurable finally only by the person who is living it. Randy Christofferson is as completely fulfilled as a high school hockey coach as he was as CEO of First USA, more so really. He's in the Zone, living once again at the intersection of his dreams and his reality. And when he's through with this time of his life, he'll step out of it into another and another, I'm sure. The beauty lies in the wave, in short, far more than in where the wave takes you.

My own guess is that no area of our lives will be more affected by this new sense of status and upward mobility than parenting. When Ask the Children, a project of the Families and Work Institute, surveyed kids to find out what they disliked most about their relationship with their parents, the answer wasn't the long hours mom and dad worked. It wasn't the absence of money or the presence of excessive discipline, or the time they got to sit or didn't get to sit in front of the TV. It was the stress that their parents brought home at the end of every workday. Kids know what makes us grownups miserable, and I honestly believe this concept of chapters, of serial reinvention, finally offers parents a clear way out of the "stress trap."

I foresee a world where each parent will routinely live chapters of perhaps three to six years where the children are the most important focus. Women will continue to become an ever more important part of the workforce, at the executive as well as the factory level—that's a given—but we won't have to make the sort of brutal all-or-nothing choices that have historically been forced on us. Rather, our lives and our husbands' and children's lives will wind around each other in these shifting waves, with primary responsibility for the kids passing back and forth as one parent heads full speed into her Zone and the other steps back and begins to plan the next chapter of his life. With our children, too, we don't have to be everything at once: soccer mom or dad, corporate senior vice president, bake-sale chairman, and so on. Instead, we can get to be all these things over the course of a child's dependent years.

We're already beginning to assemble a body of pioneers here, too, people who bear emulation. For 15 years, Randy and Judy Christofferson lived the life of a textbook corporate couple. Randy left the house at 4:30 in the morning on weekdays and rarely got back before midnight—that was the price of being on the fast track. Judy, meanwhile, was busy all the time, seeing to the house and meals and all the multiple needs of their four children. Now Randy is buying the groceries, transporting the kids, making dinner, giving Judy the chance to take a nap if that's what she wants or to get into the workplace. Plenty of other couples are doing the same thing: moving from chapter to chapter in a dance so that as one wears down and is ready to plot a new trajectory, the other can step forward into a Zone of her

> Use your coupleship creatively, and each parent can have a chapter with the kids. Dads want in, and kids win when parents find fulfillment.

own. And because they have the time to contemplate where they will go next, they're not just repeating their cycles but moving forward with them as well.

I've long felt the ideal situation would be to have one spouse building wealth through equity while the other teaches or otherwise marries his or her schedule to the kids' school hours. However you structure it, though, what matters is that the collective rhythm of your lives and your kids' lives is the same. Childhood is tough. Kids have to make enormously complicated moral choices. There are developmental issues to be seen to. As they get older, they often need more of your time, not less of it, as working mothers everywhere are now discovering. The more you can align the waves of your own life with the life cycles of your children, the easier it all will be.

Just as important, I think the workplace is going to adjust to these patterns because it can and because it has to and, once again, because we all have the words now to discuss these matters. As recently as a decade or two ago, you simply couldn't climb off the corporate—or law or medical or whatever—ladder without paying a huge price. Today, the workplace is much more like a souk, filled with great stalls and small ones, with back alleys that meander in every direction.

Not long ago the entrepreneurship department at the Harvard Business School surveyed the school's female graduates. Forty percent of those who had received their degrees at least 10 years earlier had stopped working for money. Instead, many of them were running community nonprofits, from PTAs to museum boards to charter schools. Were they interested in returning to the business world, the survey asked? Yes, the typical answer went, but they wanted to work only three days a week, for no more than seven hours a day, with time off for their kids' vacations.

For them, the paradigm of success is far closer to Judy Corman than it is to a traditional CEO. Judy cut her teeth running public relations for Epic Records and RCA. When she was in her early thirties, you could still see her occasionally standing on tables at rock concerts, screaming "Elvis lives!" When her kids were young, Judy left the record business and opened a small string of children's stores in the Hamptons, on Long Island, so she could spend more time close to home. As the kids grew, she moved on to become head of corporate communications for Phoenix House, the world's largest substance abuse center. Now she's helping run Scholastic Press, where she's played a major role in launching one of the most successful children's books series in publishing history: Harry Potter. Not only has Judy lived her life as a wave, modulating it to the needs of her family; she's been able to pull all the elements together into what finally amounts to a beautiful harmony.

When he was a Harvard Business School professor, Jeff Bardach specialized in the future of work and in the new, often implicit contracts workers were forging with their employers. Now that he's heading up Bridgespan, Bain's new consulting group formed to work solely with nonprofits, Jeff is getting to see that contract in action. Hardly anyone who works under him shows up from nine to five, Jeff told me. They're all striking their own deals, all trying to find out who they are, all making up lives on the fly.

Dayton Ogden, chairman of Spencer Stuart, the global executive recruiting firm, was talking with me the other day about this whole changing notion of coming in and out of the workplace. He sees a growing flexibility among his clients, which include many of the world's great corporations. Companies are beginning to realize they have to learn to make themselves as fluid as the best talent they seek. The key, Dayton said, is not to drop out completely if you can avoid it. Consult two days a week, do some writing or teaching—whatever it takes, keep your hand in your area of competence if that's what you want to return to. It's not the quantity of output that counts in these situations. It's the quality and the ability to demonstrate that your skills are still current in a world of rapid change.

I prided myself on being a great mom while building a great Internet company and taking it public. I spent almost all of my weekend time with my girls even if I worked late into Sunday night once they had been put to bed. I had dinner with them five nights a week, even when I went out later, and breakfast with them, too, although generally I had been up working for several hours before they even stirred. I made all the school plays. I even skipped the first half of my first shareholders meeting so I could make Michaela's, my oldest's, first recital. As far as I was concerned, my girls and I had it pretty much knocked. In this last year, though, as I've stepped away from the CEO's role and into my new skin, I see so clearly how much I had been missing.

Then, I was never out of my entrepreneurial Zone: Stress followed me like a heat-seeking missile wherever I went. Now that I'm working only 40 hours a week—keeping my hand in the fields that interest me as Dayton Ogden advises, speaking and writing, exploring with interesting people—my relationship with my kids has been transformed. In my iVillage days, I used to fantasize about renting a small studio apartment in my building so I could chill out for just five minutes before encountering the onslaught of love that was always waiting for me just on the other side of my door. Now, I rush straight through that door full speed when my workday is done, and I relish having the kids and the puppy pile on and over me. When I wake up, nothing is pressing on my mind so completely that I can't give myself over to those moments of warm cuddling that are every parent's fondest memory. And on Sunday evenings—blessed Sunday evenings!—I don't have those creeping moments of anxiety as the cares of the workweek begin to rear their ugly heads.

This sweet in-between time isn't forever, I know, even though I find myself resisting that knowledge more and more. It's not even for the rest of the girls' childhoods, although until the youngest is 18 and out the door to college, I intend to fashion at least part of my chapters to her needs. Dual parents in some ways have it easier: They have more human hours between them. In some ways, they have it harder, too: I have to compromise only with myself. But whether we're in a one-parent or a two-parent family, our kids have told us what's wrong. We need to listen to them.

Last year, I spoke to a group of female employees at Goldman Sachs, a roomful of maybe 100 women, among the best and brightest in the business. I was talking about this challenge of balancing kids and being in the Zone. There are these painful choices to make, I said. By way of illustration, I told them the whole story about Michaela's recital—not just how I missed part of the first shareholders meeting so I could be there but also how mad some of my handlers had been at me and how mad Michaela was, too. Anxious to give both sides of my life a piece of me, I'd made only part of the recital, rushing back to the meeting before it was over. By the end of my talk, I think half the women in the room were crying. We don't want to discuss these issues, but they run incredibly deep. I'd ripped open the taboo, and it was as if I had talked about death.

Teach the Children

The greatest concern I had during my last iVillage road show, when I was working day and night to sell the idea of the company to major investors, wasn't whether our IPO would be successful. The greatest concern was the time away from my girls. Physically, I was gone for two 5-day stretches. Mentally, I left them for a solid 12 days, my longest absence ever. How do you explain such things to kids, I wondered? And how can you ever expect a five-year-old to understand the concept of an initial public offering?

The answer, I know now, is that kids can understand almost anything in their own terms. When I came home the afternoon of our IPO—after spending the morning on the trading floor and later celebrating the milestone with our employees—Michaela greeted me at the door with words I'll never forget: "Mommy, Mommy," she shouted, her face absolutely lit up with excitement, "you did something so great that everyone wants to say thank you!" Then she led me into a living room full of 25 incredible bouquets, gifts from friends, colleagues, customers, board members, even an old high school teacher.

Use your coupleship creatively, and each parent can also find the Zone. Yes, you'll have fewer hours each day for your children when you're there, but they'll get to see you at the height of creativity and contribution. Isn't this a part of what we wish for them?

In that moment, too, I realized something else: It's a great thing for our children to see us in the Zone because that's where the great things we want our children to accomplish get done time and again. Far too often, we hide the details, even the texture, of our work lives from our children. Historically, at least, I think we've done it partially out of embarrassment: the sense that if our children saw how repetitious our workdays — and weeks and months and years — were, they would run for the hills as fast as their legs would carry them. That was never wholly the case, of course, but it doesn't need to be the case at all anymore. A life of serial reinvention is a life of constant discovery. It's a life of great highs and quiet times between to prepare us for whatever is next. Part of the new social contract, I'm convinced, will include an obligation to show our children all that: to let them see us at the height of our creative and leadership powers, not to shut them out when we're going through that sense of falling that so often follows great accomplishment, to let them walk through the desert with us (at their own pace, with what they can understand) as we listen to our inner voices and discover our new deep stirrings.

Joanne Lipman tells of an experience much like mine. Her daughter had a homework assignment that asked her to list women who had achieved firsts in history: "Florence Nightingale," her daughter answered, "and Joan of Arc, and in the year 2000 *The Wall Street Journal* named its first woman deputy managing editor — my Mom!" Behind all that pride, I'm certain, lay an understanding of how hard Joanne had worked for it and what she had had to give up elsewhere in her life to get there.

Things come in seasons, our children need to know. Some seasons carry us away from them for a period into a

Zone where they can never join entirely with us; other seasons bring us back to them richer people in all sorts of ways. The more we can prepare our children for that, the more they can be ready to ride these waves when their own time comes; and the more we can include them in the conversation as they get older and can understand more, the better off we all will be.

When I was only 22 and just finishing up college, I found myself interested in film, health care, a dozen other potential careers, and unable to choose between any of them. Instead, I went to the mountains out of default, to avoid what my parents kept insisting would be a 40-year choice. Happily, it was the right guess, and what began as a refuge became a chapter I wouldn't trade for anything. But because I was unable to see that my life could be a sequence of choices, not a single choice forever, I was unable to visualize anything else. The other week I overheard my six-year-old telling a friend she wanted to be an astronaut. A minute or so passed until she got back to the subject. "Now," she said, "I get to pick four other things!"

Teach your children to live in chapters, and "What do you want to be when you grow up?" will become a meaningless question—or it will take them half a day to answer.

I know why it happened: She had been watching the piles of paper that became this book grow and grow. In the way of six-year-olds, she would ask me what I was doing, and I would tell her as simply and as best I could that when she grows up, she might get to be four or five things, not just one. My wish for both my girls, and for all children, is that when they get to be 22 as I once was, they'll see the same multitude of paths in front of them that I saw, but they'll also know what I didn't: that with patience and time and careful planning, they can explore all the sides of themselves, discover which several they might want to express, and follow each of them into the conjunction of their dreams and their lives.

Our kids need to come out of not just college but high school with a sense of their unchanging and defining building blocks. They need to know that they are made up of many pieces, each of which can be expressed in many ways. Holly Hicks-Opperman of Career and Life Learning Systems e-mailed me recently to recount a conversation with her 16-year-old daughter. Holly had been talking about the chapters she still planned to lead in her own work life when her daughter interrupted her: "'What's so new about that? I plan to have at least five successful careers.' She then rattled them off: fashion designer, psychologist, actor, race-car driver, and one yet to be determined." This is a high schooler who understands the incredible richness of choice that lies ahead of her.

Just like grown-ups, kids also need to understand this new language of change so that they don't get stuck in the space between unfamiliar words. First they learn the words. Then they learn the markers the words point to. And then they learn how to navigate in a world where nothing holds still and, more important, where things don't need to hold still, including their own aspirations. My oldest daughter was very attached to my former job: She loved seeing the iVillage logo whenever it appeared; she was proud that I was a boss in a world still top-heavy with men. She also saw me go through the whole process of angst and sadness that marks the end of any chapter. And she saw me emerge into a new chapter and a new life rhythm that left far more time for her and her sister.

Now, instead of searching for iVillage logos, she comes in to my office and weighs in her little hand these growing stacks of paper, and thus she learns not just how a book is made but how change is accomplished, how it can hurt, and how we can come through it into a renewed sense of purpose and desire. She's seeing creation at work. As I begin to put the brushstrokes on this new life, Michaela will see a company, maybe more than one, forming across our dining room table.

Forget the hockey sticks. This life looks more like a wave function than an upward-trending line. The beauty is in the totality, not in the steady rise.

That's how we'll build excellence in the future, I'm convinced: by teaching our children through our own words and actions so that they can operate in the Zone again and again.

The End of Networking

When I see young professionals networking as if their lives depend upon it, I want to grab them by the shoulders and tell them: Look, if you are going to go through serial careers and a wide variety of jobs—and you probably are whether you want to or not if you're going to find true happiness and success—then just think for a second about what you're doing. It's impossible at any stage of a serial work life to say whom you will want to know 10 years from now, impossible to say even what you might need to know, and yet here you are, exhausting yourself before the chase has ever begun in earnest. Read books. Develop yourself intellectually instead of networking like crazy. You'll get much more out of it in the end.

Great work chapters like great book chapters grow organically. They flow where the next word, the next plot turn, the next revelation of character leads you. Give yourself over to that flow, and a network of customers, colleagues, bosses, luminaries, coaches, and others will naturally begin to develop around you in the normal order of doing business. Central to this whole point, it will be a network uniquely geared to this moment and chapter in your life. Even more central, it will be a network built around your present and future, not one supporting your past.

> Forget networking, too. Put your faith and energy in organic connections between mutual passions. Between passions, stay home and read good books.

Grace Park had a great law degree (Harvard). She had joined a great law firm. In theory, she should have fallen into a network that would have sustained her through a senior partnership and perhaps even high government service. But Grace's network and credentials were all about where she had come from, not where she was going. Grace had felt pressure from her father to go to law school, pressured by him and by her own success at school and the expectations it raised to join the sort of firm she did. Once she admitted to herself that practicing law held no charm for her, Grace found herself in effect almost imprisoned by her blue-chip background. It wasn't until she set out to interview people who had combined their training in the law with an interest in media and business—the cluster of interests that attracted her—that Grace was able to build a network that she had any real organic link to, and then the network just formed around her.

"Your accomplishments are the light emanating from you that attracts people," Barry Diller once told me, and he's right. Live fully in the moment, do this job and this chapter well, make a great contribution, and the molecules will begin to form around you. Accomplished people like other accomplished people. They're drawn to one another, whatever the field of endeavor, and as they are drawn together, they form their own webs that are all the more powerful because they are all the more focused.

Lois Smith is a public relations legend today, with a star-studded list of actors and actresses as clients, but the whole business got launched toward greatness because years ago she had noticed an unheralded actor playing in a Broadway production of *Barefoot in the Park* and approached him to ask if he would work with her. The two of them have been together ever since. When he helped present Lois with a major award not long ago, the actor—Robert Redford—referred to her not as his PR agent but as his "fellow traveler. . . . You see who has been by your side all the time." That kind of connection, built around a clearly defined common purpose and shared desires, will trump networking every time.

My own greatest networks don't go back to Harvard and Stanford. They grew around winning an Emmy and the Matrix Award; they sprouted up because I was invited to forums of people with the same passions I have, places like the Renaissance weekends with their obsession with family. When you become passionate about something, you will find the right people, and you'll have a real reason to get to know them and to form a reciprocal relationship with them. But all that begins with showing up and doing great things and delivering as promised. That's how you build a network that counts.

A final advantage of these ad hoc, organic networks: They disappear of their own accord once a chapter ends. Those 3,000 names I discovered in my Rolodex once I stepped back from iVillage were, in fact, a network. If I had carried all those names forward, I would have suffocated. Networks imply reciprocity: If you call me, I'll call you back; if I need your help, you're expected to give it. That's simply too many people, and too much time away from the people who need you most.

Part of this new social contract, I think, is an inherent recognition that the fluidity that applies to our lives and careers applies to these webs of associations, too. We aren't obligated forever, and we can't be. We get to pick and choose as we pick and choose our way through adulthood. All of us need that deep inner core of friends (see Circles of Associations on page 232) that Dan Lewis talks about (and that I value more and more with each passing year): Mine consists of six to eight people I know would be at the hospital day and night if I or one of my girls was lying there in critical condition. Beyond that, the next in a series of ever-widening concentric circles, comes another 15 to 20 people, representatives from every chapter I've lived through whom I expect to be close to throughout the rest of my life. These are the people who showed up at Dan's fortieth birthday party and gave him the confidence to make the move to the West Coast that so enhanced his life. They are also the ones you need to pay attention to when you're lost in the Zone and oblivious to so much that lies outside the immediate pursuit of your specific dream. Outside that are another 75 people you want to continue to know even as your focus changes because their intelligence and spiritual strength and simple decency transcends the boundaries chapters impose. My list includes John Hagel,

David Beirne, Sherry Turkle, Georgette Mosbacher, Deepak Chopra, Ruth Porat, Jim Taylor, Harriet Rubin, John O'Neil, and many more of my own spectacular fellow travelers.

That's it. That's what I can tend to. That's all the reciprocity I have the time or energy to deliver. Already as I work on this book, I can feel a new network growing around me, three dozen people I've met effortlessly because my rising interests so clearly coincide with their own. Those three dozen will lead me to six dozen more, and those to dozens upon dozens more as I move ever-more fully into this new Zone. In time, a handful of those people will osmose into my circle of 75 and from there to my circle of 20. People drop out of our lives for all sorts of reasons, and this network like all the others I've been a part of will dissolve and become yet another element in the fabric of my building life.

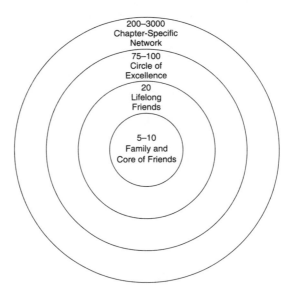

Circles of Associations

CHAPTER TEN

Leading in the New Workplace

*No story is the same after a lapse of time,
or rather, we who read it are no longer
the same interpreters.*

—George Eliot

When I was at American Express, from 1983 to 1989, the company was king; the hierarchy was unassailable; the dress code was inviolate (for women, Tiffany gold earrings and navy-blue suits); and the annual reviews by which your fealty to the crown was judged were flat-out terrifying. Amex had a star system. The stars had mentors who brought them along inch by inch, year by year. And the whole mentoring process could move at a snail's pace because everyone assumed that all the stars would be there for decades to come. Amex, after all, was at the center of the universe. The name on the building said as much: World Financial Center. Who could imagine leaving?

My job there as a young MBA was to learn the ropes, do good, and, once I had filled in enough bullet points on enough McKinsey-like presentations, get promoted and join the star club myself. Every year then chairman Lou Gerstner chose a new assistant from among those clamoring at the gate. The post was a prime one; Lou inspired and challenged us all. I still remember one of the winners: Abby Kohnstam, now Lou's head of communications at IBM—lean, quiet, Tiffany-clad and impeccably tailored, totally noncontroversial, bright as all get-out, and very, very talented. That was the ideal, and the ideal was where I set my sights.

Six years later, I dropped out of that Zone, my story line changed, and beginning in 1989, I found myself at Time Warner, where it looked as if the inmates had been handed the keys to the asylum. At Amex, authority was not to be questioned. At Time Warner, rainmakers and young editors still wet behind the ears had enormous power to make creative products and leverage demands. Where I had come from, they all would have been fired. Where this new wave had brought me, they were the "bright employee" paradigm.

In part, this was the difference between corporate cultures: Amex had emerged from the rock-steady world of New York financial institutions. The old Christian missionary zeal of Time, meanwhile, had just been merged with the feisty Jewish-Hollywood heritage of Warner Brothers. At American Express, points were what you charged credit card holders on their overdue balances. At Time Warner, points had just become a percentage of gross. Big difference. But the times were also changing, and I was living in the center of an overthrow in work values.

I joined the tech sector in 1995 as a start-up CEO. There, not only were the inmates in charge, but the normal laws of gravity seemed to have been suspended, too. Amex was the world I was taught to expect by the Harvard Business School. Time Warner had been a shock to my carefully programmed system, but this—this was a revolution. Twenty-four-year-olds, young men and women who only a decade earlier had been playing in youth soccer leagues, would barge into my office, lay their "strategic plans" on my desk, and tell me in no uncertain terms that if I didn't "get it," they were heading straight across the street to the highest bidder.

Stunned if not quite chastened, I sent up an SOS and dove into research that eventually led me to an invaluable document: "Rocking the Ages," a must-read study by Yankelovich Partners on the three generations now in the workplace: "matures," "boomers," and "xers," the study calls them, each with its own set of motivations, values, and commitments. I was in a sector where boomers like me were already old and the matures among us were mostly figurehead CEOs brought on board to make major investors more comfortable. The xers were the ones I needed to come up to speed on, and in a hurry—they were already changing the culture of the workplace almost beyond recognition—and Yankelovich had them dead-on.

Generation Restless

Having seen their parents crushed by corporations to whom they had given years of their lives, sometimes with little reward at the end, the xers had given up on loyalty. Loyalty, their evidence suggested, bought you a lifetime of missed moments—the high school basketball games never attended, the first boyfriends never met, the family vacations cut short or canceled altogether at the whim of distant corporate masters. Whatever else they might be, xers had determined never to be owned in the same way, and the full-employment economy of the middle and late 1990s, especially in the Internet space I was then living in, had given them the luxury and room to turn their determination into practice. America and the world were full of opportunities for bright 24-year-olds. Venture capital was circling overhead, looking for a place to land. We boomers, matures, and worse could like it or lump it—this wasn't a climate to foster modesty, of character or ambition. And fine I say to all that, really . . . except for one thing: The xers I was reading about and working among seemed to know what they didn't want, but they also seemed destined to never experience the rewards of deep commitment. Instead of the Zone, instead of the passion that comes with the realization of great aspiration, xers had restlessness.

Armed with at least the outlines of their philosophy, I spent hours and hours talking with our iVillage xers about all this. What did they want out of life? What were they willing to make sacrifices for? What were their ideals? Who were the employee paradigms in their own minds? What were the warning signs that resonated with them? The bright lines they knew they would never cross over? These weren't formal meetings. We were all stripped down to our shirtsleeves, engaged in a cross-generational dialogue that was really about reinventing the nature of work. Finally, after what seemed a thousand pizzas and dozens upon dozens of late evenings added to the long hours we were already putting in, a new path did begin to develop, a process that would allow the best

of our in-house xers to experience deep commitment without feeling trapped by it in a corporate enclave that they wor-
ried would ultimately screw them as other enclaves had
screwed their moms and dads. I was shocked at how deeply
those scars went, but I was surprised, too, by how anxious
these young people really were to let their longtime aspirations blossom. And I knew that if we could do that and put
their desires to work for iVillage, it would be a win-win situation all around.

I've described the program that emerged from all this in
pieces elsewhere in this book. Let me put it down here in formal fashion with the warning that it was created by trial and
error and is still a work in progress. Not all of our workforce
took part initially: Our first concern had been with top talent, 20 percent of the whole, although I later opened it up to
anyone who wanted to take part. A few of those who threatened to jump ship if they didn't get a go-ahead on their strategic plans did jump, despite our "third way," although more
than a few of them called me later—new grads of the school
of hard knocks—to acknowledge that following their plans
would have been a disaster. What follows, in short, isn't
gospel, but I believe something like it is the future of the new
workplace because only through this or some similar plan can
employers bring themselves fully into synch with the talent
that always makes the difference.

The program we ultimately created at iVillage had four
steps, each of which flowed from a single question:

1. *What's your personal mission statement?* The idea isn't
   new—Stephen Covey introduced the mission statement
   in his best-selling *Seven Habits of Highly Successful*

People—but I've never yet found a better shorthand for getting people to address their own deepest aspirations. Until you do that, until you go deep within and hear what the voices are saying—including the voice that's reading your own obituary—everything else is just paying the rent. The trick is to be honest and to insist on honesty and, hardest of all, to confront people when you think they're falling short of being honest with themselves. When I brought our senior team together to do this exercise, I was aware that several of them had allowed their personal and work lives to drift apart. As we ended up, I looked around the room and saw one of the people I had been concerned about—a woman seemingly invulnerable to emotion—with tears streaming down her cheeks. Three months later, she made a major change in her career to bring these aspects of her life into alignment.

To maximize contribution, maximize self-awareness. Each worker's unique attributes, gifts, preferences, and temperament are the most solid basis for matching individuals and jobs in a tumultuous world.

2. *What's your dream job?* Forget about whether it seems attainable. *Remember:* The worst thing you can do in this change-driven world is pre-edit your desires. The Williams sisters got to be Wimbledon champs because they were willing to risk walking into the dream of excellence that their father had shown them, just as a carpenter gets to be great because he has the courage to walk into his own dream of perfect joints and corners. At iVillage, we were careful to note that the position didn't

have to exist within our company—this was about under-standing themselves, not applying for someone else's slot. (About one in three women said their dream job would be being Oprah, a position we didn't have open.) Once they had identified what job would be the realization of their own dreams, we asked our stars to interview some-one who now held it or a similar position.

3. *Based on the interview, what 20 skills will get you to that dream job, and which ones of the 20 do you lack?* Without thinking big, you'll never step back to see the big picture, and absent that, you'll never think as realistically as you need to about what can get you from here to there. You make your own luck by being hard-nosed about what would make your dreams come true. Those who went through our program rated themselves on each skill on a five-point scale; when they were through, we asked their peers within the company to refine the ratings. As a rule, their peers gave them significantly lower mastery marks. One classically restless xer who daily resented not being a CEO by the time he was 27 rated himself as having 10 of the 20 necessary skills. His peers gave him high marks on only five skills, the beginning of both humility and learning, and also just about the average for all partici-pants once the back and forth was over.

4. *Of the skills you now lack, what positions and responsi-bilities within this company would help you gain a mas-tery of them?* We worked with the participants to leverage the skills they had mastered into a position where they could master as many more. Then they could leverage those into yet another position and so on. Don't just get

the skill, we told them: Excel at it. Soon, you'll find that an abstract route to a dream job is becoming a finely grained map.

Our goal from the beginning was to create a process of self-discovery that would allow our best talent to engage fully with their own dreams while also increasing their immediate and future contribution to the company. We wanted to align their skills and values and, critically, their aspirations, with the work they did for us, and we meant for that discussion to be explicit, not behind closed doors with senior management excluded. Now, when our best people were offered other jobs with higher pay or more glamorous titles—and that happened all the time—they had a solid context inside which to assess the offer. Would the offer enhance my ultimate marketability or retard it? Would it get me closer to the skills I need so I can enter the Zone I now know is for me? Or would it take me further away from where the deep voices were telling me I want to be? Merely getting ahead, our process said in word and deed, wasn't the point. Getting where you really wanted to go, and getting there on your own steam at your pace on your own timetable via your own definition of success, mattered for far more.

It seems simple in retrospect, but we wanted our best people to feel free to stay as well as to go, free to commit instead of just free to move on and on and on in the nomadic manner of restless xers. We knew our relationship was ultimately temporary. That's the way of the world today, especially for top talent. But the more people we had working in the Zone, the more we could maximize their output while they were with us, and the more they felt the thrill of deep commitment, the more they would move on to great success wherever they went next. Better four to five years of great output than ten to fifteen mediocre ones: better for us and better for them. Strangely, too, as we dropped loyalty out of the equation, it began to reemerge on its own: based now not on an expectation of a lifetime association but on the sense the company had shown regard for and real value in helping people achieve their deepest longings.

> Give your employees a pension plan, and you've fed them. Help them combine their missions, values, and dream job with the skills needed to achieve it, and you've taught them to feed themselves.

In truth, it's still amazing to me how well it worked. We had a mission at iVillage that it was easy to dedicate yourself to and take pride in. We were pioneers. We were doing good, providing an incredibly useful service to women as well as changing the terms of the dialogue between women and advertisers. And for a while we were also generating paper wealth faster than a mushroom flush. All that helped. But what really helped was that we made our company as fluid as our future stars were already sensing the workplace and their work and personal lives have to be.

Even when our paths diverged, we still had a basis for conversation that helped make most separations clean and amicable. Again, we had the words, and once we had the words, we could articulate to one another the thoughts behind them. As a direct result, I'm convinced, iVillage has had a terrific experience with people who have left the company, tried a chapter elsewhere, and then come back again. We held the door wide open for them.

My good friend Elysia spent eight highly productive years with a leading media company before deciding to call it quits. At the end of her tenure, the company had a new business and a broad strategy to guide it. By my lights, that should be a cause for celebration: for what she had done and for her having the good sense to move on when she felt entropy begin to settle in. Who doesn't deserve praise for realizing, against so many obstacles, when the observation point that Jonas Salk identified has arrived? Instead, Elysia got the silent treatment from her boss: So long. Don't call us, we'll call you. Slam! As Silicon Valley learned early on, real talent is too precious to alienate like that on the way out the door because you might want the same talent back under your roof before the year is out. Talent shortage or not, it also sends a horrible message back down the line. Like workers, employers need to honor exits, not just entrances. We need to recognize that a great departure is every bit as valuable as a great arrival.

As Rosabeth Moss Kanter speaks of in *Evolve!*, assumptions of "blind loyalty" must be replaced by the notion of freely "renewable commitment."

Radical Mentoring

One more thing we did at iVillage: We developed an accelerated learning curve that we called "radical mentoring." An adult work life will always be a long run, I believe, but instead of resembling a marathon, most work lives in the future—and maybe most already today—are more in the nature of wind sprints: short, sharp bursts of speed, punctuated by time in between to rest and get your strength and wind back. The 20-year mentoring system made sense at the Amex I had worked for: No one was going anywhere, except up the ladder. At iVillage, by the mid-1990s, it was quickly apparent that such a system made no sense at all. We had entered an age in which company strategies have shorter tenures and require reinvention far more quickly. So do the people who implement them, and the higher the talent level, the shorter their tenure is likely to be.

If you're going to have an ace employee for, say, four to six years instead of the old gold standard of twenty, how do you maximize his contribution to the organization? And how do you justify the always high cost of bringing talent to maturity? Our answer was tied to the four-part process already described. Once a high performer had identified her aspirations, more specific ambitions, and the skills she thought she needed and lacked, a mentor would invite her to work with him for six months, to address those areas—rarely more than three or four in number—where a breakthrough would have an exponential effect, catapulting the person forward in a matter of months as opposed to a matter of years or decades under the old mentoring regime. Instead of annual or semiannual evaluations, our mentees got feedback three or four times a day, maybe for only a few min-

> The old mentoring model is dead. Loyalty in the new workplace will be gained by pointing people toward *their* dreams, not toward *our* dreams for them.

utes at a time but clearly directed to the issues they were working on, at the time they were working on them.

In a sense, we went down into the flow with the people we were mentoring. We jumped in the river with them, and the results were explosive. Among the early people we brought through the process was a young marketing assistant who became one of the founders of our first international brand, iVillageUK. There was also a Web-channel producer to whom we offered the chief operating officer's slot 18 months after she had entered the radical mentoring program as an alternative to being fired. Under the old calendar, such bump-ups just wouldn't have been possible. Under the new one, they were happening all around us.

One large Midwestern nonprofit had been divided for years into three divisions. When the executive committee decided the group needed more fresh blood flowing through its veins, it turned those three divisions into 30 focus units and posted all 30 unit leader jobs within the organization. In all, about 95 people applied for the slots, and 30 of those were chosen to lead the new units. Not surprisingly, the three former division leaders freaked out. Who were they now? What was going to be done with all the experience they had accumulated? The answer: Each picked 10 of the new focus-unit heads and became, in essence, their full-time mentor. The group arrived at radical mentoring through the back door, but it got there all the same, and by doing so it let loose energies that were begging to be exploited.

Rigor Mortis

Dee Soder, one of the leading CEO "coaches" in the country, has told me that only about one in five of top executives has the inner fluidity and capacity for change that I have been describing in this book. Far more often than not, she said, the top corporate brass seeks out predictable situations and work to build a predictable and constant structure within which to operate. For many of them, Dee went on, the crisis point tends to come about 15 years out, especially if they have stayed in a single environment, even when they have held a variety of posts within it. By then, they're likely to find the winds of change howling at their door, no matter how hard they've worked to seal themselves inside. Worse, a kind of rigor mortis has set in that makes them significant hiring risks, no matter how talented.

Dayton Ogden, the chairman of Spencer Stuart, told me much the same thing, from the opposite side of the hiring equation. The ideal candidate for a top corporate position today, Dayton said, has multiple chapters of high responsibility and achievement, each of roughly five to seven years. Rather than being the mark of a corporate hobo, such a résumé signals an ability and, even more important, a willingness to master change across a wide variety of environments.

Many of the best boards of directors have been intuiting the same message: In a world of constants, constancy is a virtue; in a world of change, it's the shortcut to stagnation. In March 2001, Hershey Foods—long one of America's most insular corporations, based in a hometown named for its founder and with a culture built powerfully around Milton Hershey's memory—went outside the corporate family for the first time in its 107-year history to name Nabisco executive Richard Lenny as its new chairman. As one analyst explained, Hershey was losing in the fight for "stomach share," in large part because too many people who had come of age in the company were interpreting "stomach share" in the same way.

"People who are attracted to and stay in a large stable company by and large are those people who are more comfortable with structure and stability," David Nadler, the chairman of Mercer Delta Consulting, told me. "That's why large companies in some industries are so hard to change. They're full of people who feel comfortable with the status quo. That's particularly true of leadership that has grown up in the company. Unless there are people inside who are particularly visionary, you need a significant importation of leadership talent to accomplish change because the people who are products of the system are the worst ones to try to lead the change."

Another example comes from Yahoo!, the company that created one of the most pervasive Internet brands. For over five years, CEO Tim Koogle and his leadership group had defined a great and cohesive management team. Their very cohesiveness, though, had become insularity, and the depth of their conviction had mutated into a liability in a rapidly altering world. Faced with mounting corporate losses, Tim stepped down and the search for an outside CEO began. In the old world, all of this would have marked a failure for Tim, but a *Wall Street Journal* account of Tim's departure recognized that this sort of change and morphing is both natural and entirely appropriate. Tim had been one of the gold standards of the business — maybe *the* gold standard — but what works in one cycle doesn't always work in the next. Growth yields to decline, start-ups tend toward maturity, the life span of corporate cultures gets truncated in the bargain, and the leaders who are just right for today are less so for tomorrow. Eventually, Tim was succeeded as CEO by Time Warner's Terry Semel, a veteran of the old media world.

At the Transitions Institute, which identifies and trains professional Navigators, David Zelman and I have been working with company founders to help them develop personal road maps that don't include the companies they created. By imagining a future for themselves apart from their companies—and just as important, a future for their companies that doesn't include them—many of the founders are finding the courage to move on 12 to 18 months in advance of the inevitable crisis points that arrive as a company grows and expands. For their companies, change gets to unfold organically, without the artificial constraints imposed by a founder who hangs on too long. The founders, meanwhile, get to move on to new challenges, to follow new dreams. They're trading in repetition for reinvention.

In the future, I'm convinced, companies and especially their boards will be judged by how clearly they see this need to encourage moving on at the top and how quickly they respond. It won't be easy. Despite tremendous strides in governance overall, cronyism is too often the name of the game in naming new board members. But boards have a primary responsibility, fiduciary and moral, to sense the change in zeitgeist because the people they are charged with overseeing have a built-in tendency to deny the early warnings of having peaked along Salk's Epic B curve.

More and more, leaders of all sorts will be judged by the same sort of yardstick, I think: not by how long they manage to hang on but by how effectively they manage to time their departure to the changing rhythms of their companies. CEOs can't afford to get out of touch with the world around them. They succeed most as leaders when they cause the culture of the company and their industry sector to gel around them, but in a change-driven world, cultures ungel as quickly as they set and move on to other ideas and other products and other interpretations of the ways to generate wealth and shareholder value. True wisdom is knowing how to let go of a position and renew your strength and find new sources of inspiration within, so you can lead again in whatever field the inner voices direct you toward.

Outplacement firms have a long way to go in this regard, too. Not surprisingly, the business of helping workers relocate has become a lucrative field in recent years; yet as generally practiced, the discipline clings to old definitions and prescriptions. Change is bad. Endings are failures. Instead of encouraging their clients to take time to look within themselves for new directions they want to pursue, many firms advise getting back on the same horse as soon as possible. In the meantime, many of them provide clients with offices just like the ones they've only recently left. The idea is to cushion the falling process, but the practical effect can be devastating. Only one in five of us feels we're in the right job to start with. Rather than use their resources to help clients contemplate dream jobs, uncover their fundamental work personality, and pursue opportunities that might produce a much better ultimate fit and thus a much higher level of ultimate success, the outplacement firms support a status quo that holds people in pasts they don't want to repeat but can't escape without true Navigators.

> The outplacement of the past is a model of narrowing options. The future is the opening of the tunnel toward greater freedom and choice.

At the Center for Executive Options, Phil Simhauser takes exactly the opposite approach. Phil had been one of the creators of the original outplacement business and had watched its limitations unfold. Today, his Center provides no offices for its clients or anything else that is intended to recreate their old position or status. Clients are encouraged to imagine a new professional life for themselves, and then the Center uses a global network of high-powered peers to help bring the new dreams to life. One high-ranking Defense Department official moved on to write a novel and now teaches organizational strategy at UCLA. A much-decorated major general became an executive at a major tobacco producer and now buys and sells companies in South America. A professional ballet dancer went from dancing on the stage to working at Xerox to teaching at the Stern Business School. An ex-Harvard Business School professor sold the pioneering venture-capital firm he had founded in Prague and bought a brokerage operation that became the basis for the Chinese stock exchange. The Center limits itself to very senior people, but its creativity is sending a message from the future to all of us.

Rigidity, I'm convinced, is the only quality that truly spells disaster these days, for careers and companies—that and failing to understand our own best environments. We don't need jobs that reinforce what others think we should be doing: That way lies suboptimal performance even for true stars. We need jobs that fit our own temperaments, lifestyle, values, and innate strengths.

The New Loyalty

At the height of the Internet boom, when normal values seemed to have been turned upside down, a 27-year-old iVillage employee walked into my office to tell me he was leaving. Why, I asked? Because, he said, he had been offered a $1 million signing bonus from another company. Fine, I said, but let's take an hour and understand this, and with that I shut the door, and we got down to business.

I wasn't surprised, of course. Plenty has been written about the forces undermining workplace loyalty, and a million dollar check at age 27 is a pretty compelling one. But as he talked, another story began to emerge. It was apparent that this employee truly loved our company. He believed in us, in our mission, and in the company we were building. The highest bidder had spoken, and in the spirit of the age, he felt he had to listen. But the decision was bringing him no joy—tears were pooling in his eyes as he spoke. Going to the highest bidder, I told him, can make you rich, but it also can enslave you. Without the mooring of loyalty of some kind, to something, no one can really be free.

What emerged out of the collapse of the old loyalty, I came to realize in that moment, was in many ways more sorrowful than what had been. Life is empty without commitment. Now, though, I think a new contract is gradually evolving—in some companies and some industries, but with momentum to spread throughout the workplace—that builds mutual loyalty on three foundations: the company mission, a commitment by the company to assist employees in optimizing their value in the marketplace, and a commitment to help employees better understand where their best fit is and where their best chances of success and fulfillment lie.

In large part, that's what we were doing at iVillage. This new workplace contract marries the corporate good with individual aspiration. Beneath that lies a larger notion: We—company and worker—will both be better off if we learn to swim with each other and if we all learn to speak a language of change that isn't freighted with old assumptions. Of all the companies he has worked with, David Nadler says that Corning is perhaps the best example of this new contract, especially in its commitment to the third leg: helping employees better understand where and what their best environment is if it turns out not to be at Corning.

"There's a phrase Corning uses," David told me when we met in his elegant Manhattan offices at 46th Street and Avenue of the Americas. "They talk about getting people repotted. It's like a plant. You pull the plant out, you put it in a different pot, and all of a sudden, the plant starts to flourish. That's what Corning is so good at.

"It's not always gentle, but it's always done compassionately. They'll take a relatively senior executive, and they'll say, 'I think you've done what you can do here,' and they'll help these people search out where they can succeed and what they want to do. One's teaching at Cornell. Another went into venture capital. And, you know, they're doing quite well. A number of them at the time felt angry and hurt, naturally, but now when I talk with them, they say, 'Boy, that's one of the greatest things to ever happen to me. I'm much happier. It's much better than it would have been to stay there.'"

> When firing is used to "repot" workers into more fertile soil, the result can be lifelong loyalty to the company that let them go.

That, too, I think, is going down to the river with your employees. That's making your flow and their flow one and the same. It's taking the language of evolution and morphing that companies today routinely apply to new generations of products and services and applying it to the humanware as well, wherever the humanware is found and whatever it's doing. Volunteer organizations can benefit as much from repotting as for-profit ones. It's not a matter of what anyone earns, if anything; it's a matter of freeing people from ingrained habits and bad fits to realize their own potential. Not every organization will or can respond the same way. Nor, certainly, will every employee. As David Nadler suggests, risk-averse workers tend to gravitate toward institutions that raise structural walls against change. But even large bureaucracies have hidden pockets of fluidity that they and their employees can tap.

One public school science teacher I know, in a huge 700,000-student system, dreamed of opening a small company that would distribute the educational videos he was using in his own classroom. He didn't want to leave the classroom; he wasn't looking to get rich. He just thought he had a better way of teaching science that ought to be shared. Finally, after days of scouring programs on his behalf, a science coordinator at the central office found a $10,000 summer grant hidden away in the audiovisual budget that could be used to launch the business. One giant step for my teacher friend: Four years later, he's still teaching, but now with more enjoyment than ever before. The grant kick-started him into his tiny business. His tiny business kick-started him into a Zone he's still living and working inside. One giant step also for breaking through the bureaucratic walls and aligning organizational commitment with individual aspiration.

Leading in the new workplace is about respecting individual paths. It's about encouraging exploration, even when it carries your best talent past your borders. It's about honoring the exits of those who should leave and making certain, to the best degree you can, that they discover in the process their own best selves. And it's about letting loose the enormous energy that goes untapped in so many workplaces. You want to access tools that will enable each employee to operate in the Zone as much of the time as possible; recognize that you can do this only when you attune your organization to the inevitable cycles of passion, peaks, entropy, and renewal that we all go through; and something new is going to happen. Just as the technological revolution unleashed fresh sources of productivity in the economy, so this revolution in the treatment of our human technology will be the basis of another great leap forward in productivity—a leap we can now only begin to imagine.

CHAPTER ELEVEN

At the Heart of All True Desire

I have begun to have an idea of life, not as the shaping of achievement to fit my preconceived ideas, but as the gradual discovery of a purpose which I did not yet know.

—Joanna Field

*B*ecause I'm an expert skier, I thought mastering snowboarding would be a snap. Wrong. Going diagonally across the slope at Aspen was easy. Snowboards have two edges, and I was on one of them—dug in, following a course, comfortable. The problem came whenever I had to turn. That meant leaving the edge, and once you do that in snowboarding, you're in free fall, strapped to a small surfboard with no control—until you find an edge again.

For the first several days I freaked out every time I had to make a turn. Once, I became so panicked 10 feet into a new slope that I froze in place and had to wait for a strong, silent type to come and haul me back up the slope again. All I wanted was to get the turns over with as quickly as possible. To make that happen, I began to develop so many bad habits that I finally found an instructor and begged him to unravel the mess.

"You've got to let yourself free fall down the hill and stay in it," he advised me. "Count to 50. Do whatever you can to hold it."

I tried, but at first, I was so uncomfortable that my stomach was doing back flips. After maybe a dozen times of doing the turns correctly, though, I began to sense that a new edge would always be waiting for me when I was through freefalling. I was going to catch it, and because I was, I was totally safe no matter how out of control I might feel at the moment. What's more, the steeper the slope I was on and the more I pointed myself directly downhill at these moments of turning, the more powerful would be my trajectory on the new curve when I finally did get back in control.

So it is with serial reinvention. The next chapter is always going to be there waiting, but the more fully we can throw ourselves into each turn between chapters, the more powerful our trajectory will be once we arrive. And the more we practice these turns, the surer we will be of the outcome. Practice not only makes perfect; it also makes us comfortable. In time, the faith in our capacity to get to the places we want to go and to be all the things we want to be in a lifetime will be so great that it will pull us forward of its own accord.

"At the heart of all true desire is spontaneous creation," Deepak Chopra writes. All that is asked of us is to want something enough to make it come true.

Dancing with Dread

Life is full of reasons not to pursue the course of action I've outlined in this book. It's easy, for example, to say that money stands in the way, and it can. The rainy-day fund my father advised me to start has come through for me time and again at these moments of turning, but I've also known many people who reinvented and redirected themselves on very modest or no reserves because they had to. My friend John Davie began his architecture career with a prestigious firm in Charleston, South Carolina. When a divorce unmoored his life, he moved 500 miles south and set up a private practice that was just beginning to pay off when an economic downturn dried up his client base and forced him to close his door. Fifty, with a new family to support and now running on nothing but fumes, John told me that he grew increasingly despondent and listless. Finally, he picked himself up again and now oversees construction for Habitat for Humanity in Jacksonville, Florida. The family lives lean in a two-bedroom home, but everyone is happy and John looks a foot taller when he walks around these days.

The critical issue is less the dollars in the bank, I'm convinced, than the determination to live fully. Do that, it so often seems, and not only can the money stretch astoundingly far; it can also begin to multiply itself in ways we never anticipate. One good friend was telling me the other day that he put off making the transition from a corporate job to consulting for four years because he simply couldn't get past this hurdle of money. "I'd do the math," he said, "and then my wife and I would sit down to try to figure what we could do without, and that would be it. Finally, we just said to hell with it. We'd bite the bullet. I quit, took six months to set up the consulting business the way I wanted it, and then hung out my shingle. Within a year, I had doubled my income. The 40- and 50-hour weeks I was working before used to wear me out. I'd sleep half the weekend. Now I'm working 60- and 70-hour weeks—hard weeks, with no coasting—and I love it. I didn't even know I had this kind of energy in me."

> Don't let money short-circuit the process. You can reset a trajectory on less than $500.

Phil Simhauser of the Center for Executive Options was telling me much the same kind of story. "Half the people who walk in here," he said, "make more money in two years once they get in touch with their dreams than they did in their last 25 years of slugging their way up the ladder." The force fields we build around us when we set out to make our fantasies come true attract all sorts of things, money included.

For many of us, sheer fear can stand in the way, too. Our natural instinct is to avoid the emotions that make us uncomfortable, and a whole slew of them—fear, confusion, envy—get unleashed at these turning points. But these are the tools of reinvention. Envy can be debilitating, or it can be a compass pointing us toward people who are on the path we are personally drawn to. Once we accept fear as the price of admission and get past it, we open up whole new arenas of possibility. The choice is really ours to make. Rather than always seek comfort, we become comfortable with discomfort.

I was never so scared in my life as I was during the three-day ascent of the Half Dome rock face at Yosemite. By day, we inched our way upward, tiny crevice and foothold by tiny crevice and foothold. I can remember overhangs where I was climbing almost upside down. At night, we slept in sleeping bags suspended from cliffs and ledges, with nothing but air between us and the hard earth a thousand feet below. Fear was all around me during that ascent, but here's the key thing: It didn't stop me or my climbing companions from getting to the top.

When Randy Christofferson arrived at Harvard Business School for his first day of classes, he had literally everything he owned in the trunk of his car. All his savings had gone to meet the tuition bill. If he failed or if it was the wrong place for him, Randy would have risked everything for no reward. He was, he said, terrified—there was no other word for it—and when he graduated two years later near the top of his class, that terror made the moment all the sweeter. Fear is noise, nothing more. It has no information value. It's not predictive.

Don't let fear short-circuit you. Once you become comfortable with discomfort, you open whole new arenas of possibility.

Part of the challenge here is to be honest, most centrally with yourself. What is it you really want to do with your time, your talent, your energy, your life? If you could live your life segment by segment, chapter by chapter, is this what you would want to be doing? It all sounds so basic, and yet it can be so very hard.

"The trick is to tell yourself the truth over time," says Bill Strickland, who has fashioned a life of serial reinvention out of his own unyielding determination to live that way. "People are so unable to tell the truth anymore. They've forgotten how to do it. It's a vocabulary, a skill set, and you relearn it by practice."

Remember, this is not going to be a life built around convenience. You're choosing the hard road because you want to. When you do that, the easy and the comfortable, even sometimes the familiar, all become casualties. But that's another thing the mountains taught me: Convenience can be way overrated. Back when I was with the National Outdoor Leadership School, I remember leading a patrol up to the top of a wild and dazzling mountain in the Cirque of the Towers just as dusk was settling in. No one in my group knew it yet, but we were going to spend the night up there without food and sleeping bags, bedded down on the rocks, with not even a fire to warm us. We were cold. We were miserable by the usual objective standards. But there wasn't a person among us who would trade that single night under the peaks of the Wind River in Wyoming for a week of cozy evenings under down comforters in the best five-star hotel in the world.

> The trick is to tell yourself the truth over time, and to stretch your capacity for inconvenience in the name of your dreams.

Holly Atkinson went through seven years of medical training, but it took her less than a year of practice to realize that doctoring wasn't for her. Driven by a desire to reach large numbers of people and help them lead better lives, Holly went back to school—this time to study journalism at Columbia University. In 1981, on the day Pope John Paul II was shot by would-be assassins, Holly went to work as a research assistant for Walter Cronkite. Her medical school friends were finally beginning to pull down large salaries and major appointments. Holly wasn't doing that—she started at $18,000 a year and spent a lot of time at first getting coffee—but her work for the famous voice of *CBS News* led to a job with a global news organization that gave her the platform she had been seeking from the start. As head of Reuters Health for 13 years, Holly globe-trotted between Hong Kong, New York, and Paris. When she married a New Yorker and became a stepmother, she had to retool again, and that's when she landed at iVillage, as president of iVillage Health, where she now uses the Internet to help more than 10 million women lead healthier lives.

Things worth doing are worth doing in and of themselves, not because they're convenient. When I adopted Ellie, I brought into my family a child with serious physical and developmental issues at the worst possible time in my professional life. The dual challenge of being Ellie and Michaela's mother and CEO of an Internet start-up was back-breaking, and the pain went on for a good two years. Do I regret it? Do I wish I hadn't adopted her? Not in the least, which is why I'm planning to adopt again. Nor do I regret going without sleep two nights a week for two and a half years in my mid-forties as we were growing iVillage. I'd do that again in a minute, too; and I will, but in a different chapter, with a different set of circumstances, in the pursuit of different goals.

Inside the Wave

Whether it's imposed by our own hand or by forces outside our control, change is going to find us in this new world.

Masters of this way of life learn to accept that, and they learn to relax into it. Like snowboarders or the practitioners of ancient transition rituals, they have come to trust totally in the outcomes, and because they do, their experience builds from transition to transition (see the Model of Success in the Twentieth Century and the Model of Success in the Twenty-First Century below).

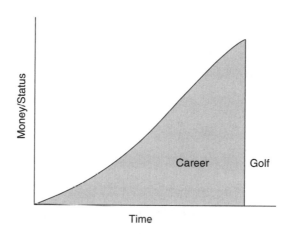

The Model of Success in the Twentieth Century

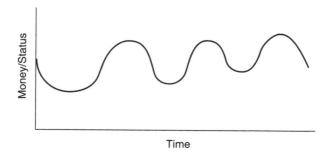

The Model of Success in the Twenty-First Century

They accept that there will be seasons of intensity and seasons of rest, not sorted into the first 65 years and a final 15 or 30, but intertwined with each other, all along the way, in an undulating curve. And they know that if they live each of these seasons fully—the ones that take them into the world and the ones that take them into themselves—they won't have to start over and nothing will be wasted. All their assets, all their belongings, are fuel. Everything they have learned in the past, all they have done before, is only preamble to what they will learn and what they will do in the years ahead.

Learn to relax into change, and change will take care of you.

Marybeth Anderson told me a remarkable story not long ago. She'd grown up an Air Force brat, living all over the place—her father had been Head Chaplain of the service—but her uncle had had horses and those became the anchor of her life. At 10, she got her first pony. When she graduated from college, she moved to Colorado, intent on getting into harness racing, but just as she got there, the state canceled the sport. With no clue what to do next, Marybeth went into underwriting commercial property in and around Denver, and from there to selling stocks and mutual funds. Everything was going great guns until the market crash of 1987. More than bursting the bubble, though, the crash told her that she had no real passion for buying and selling.

Marybeth moved to Morrison, a tiny Colorado mountain town, for six months to figure out what to do next. When her money ran out and the 4 feet of snow outside her front door made her stir-crazy, she moved back to Denver and answered a want ad from a video production company that needed to raise money. One thing led to another—a succession of producer and development jobs that continually interwove her new interests in film and her old experience with money. Today, Marybeth is an event producer who uses video, film projections, and much more to create corporate events for clients like Pepsi and High Prairie Farm, one of the leading equestrian centers in the world. Marybeth is helping oversee a handicapped partners program for High Prairie and a new, nationally prominent horse park that features a research facility to study the effect of horses on the impaired, particularly kids. She's back, in short, almost to where she began, but with a far richer mix of skills and experiences. Everything comes together if we let it.

"Failure Constructed Me"

Serial living isn't movement for movement's sake. All this can be done within a single industry, a single career, a single job. What matters is that your outer and inner selves are in alignment and that they are allowed to grow together, and to grow along with the outer and inner selves of those you love and want to spend your life with. Do that, and you won't be starting over time and again. You'll be constantly building on what is already there, and the world will honor and respect you for the effort, wherever it may carry you.

Loren Stell still amazes me. His passage from seminary to journalism, his desire to write despite his dyslexia, his long years of frustration and his growing fascination with fairy tales, how he built on that to launch himself as a therapist and how he now uses fairy tales, poetry, and dream analysis to help his clients is an object lesson for all of us in serial living and in how the strings of our lives pull together if only we allow them to do so. When I met with Loren in the elegant but intensely personal office where he sees his patients, I asked what he saw as the lessons in his own life, and he told me this story by way of explanation:

"I was listening to a program on BBC about Roger Banister, the great miler who became a doctor. Banister was saying that he had been both a runner and med student when he went to Europe to compete in an all-European meet. He was the best, he said, the fastest runner in England then, but he went to that meet and finished twelfth in the mile, and when he came home, the headlines all read: 'Banister—Give It Up. Go Back to Medical School.' That sort of thing, so he did, but he also began this new training regimen built around sprints. He would force himself to run a timed sprint, walk a little bit, then do another timed sprint—one after the other, time and again, with just a little rest between. After he'd done that for a while, he went to another race and became the first person ever to beat the four-minute mile. Afterwards, someone asked him how he did it, and he said, 'I never would have done it if it hadn't been for that failure in Europe.'

"I feel the same," Loren went on. "I feel that my failure constructed me. That's why I'm here right now, I think: because I failed big."

In a life like Loren's—one that is always building, never completed—our failures are as important as our successes in setting the trajectory of our future.

At the Matrix Awards dinner the other week, I was humbled by the caliber of the women on the dais and proud to be among the alumnae. Two common threads ran through the acceptance speeches that evening: Careers are, in fact, messy affairs, with more meanderings, lost years, and unexpected turns than we generally like to acknowledge. Winner after winner told tales of being fired or otherwise derailed, often at the worst time, but they also said that, like Loren Stell, it is possible to turn all this into grist for a life of exhilaration and accomplishment. And their own presence on the dais offered all the evidence necessary that this was so.

As if to reinforce the point, a few days later I had dinner with a woman named Lynda who has been in the publishing industry for the last two decades. She likes stability, Lynda said, and over 20 years she had managed to build a career within her company that presented her with a series of fresh challenges. In the inimitable way of the twenty-first century, though, it was all about to end. Six months earlier, her husband of 10 years had been offered what for him was a dream job in the film business. The job, though, was in San Francisco, where Lynda's position simply wasn't replicable. Now, she has to enter the dance she has managed to avoid for so long.

Lynda was, I could see, on the brink of the same sort of panic that I had felt snowboarding a few months earlier, and all I could do was tell her what my instructor had told me then: Go with the experience. Don't try to pull yourself out of it prematurely. You will find an edge, and when you do, you'll have the full power of your fall to send you into a new trajectory. Loss isn't always bad, for people or for companies. Like the Web—the defining metaphor of our

The Zone is only the visible tip of the iceberg. The quality of the gaps between chapters determines the quality of the Zones when you are living fully in them.

time—we flow together, draw strength and knowledge from one another, and flow apart again, perhaps to reconnect at some other place, in some other time that none of us can predict right now. That's the way the world is. We need to accept it on its own terms and use it to our own advantage.

Masters of Freedom

Of all the people I know, my friends Glenn and Meg might be the most successful at having aligned this process of reinvention with the rhythms of their own lives. Glenn came out of the rough projects of New York's South Bronx. It was a Jesuit priest, Glenn says, who finally told him, "You're going to have to choose how you want to live." Glenn did. He straightened himself out, went to college on an athletic scholarship, and from there went on to IBM in the early seventies, when Big Blue was the hot place to be.

Glenn had signed on as a systems engineer, but early on at IBM he was placed in a program meant to teach people throughout the organization each other's function. Every time their mastery was tested in the program, Glenn found himself scoring off the charts, not in his own discipline but in sales and marketing, so he moved into that and eventually left the company, after six years, to spend another thirteen years in magazine ad sales, shuttling between Hearst and Conde Nast, and doing terrifically at both.

Meg, by contrast, had grown up on a farm, gone off to college and IBM, where she met and married Glenn, and from there went to business school and into commercial real estate for six years. When their first child was born, she took a year off, learned that working was her way, and went back to full-time employment, this time on the trading desk of a major investment bank, a monstrously intense job but one with iron-clad hours that allowed her to get home in time to share dinner with a growing family.

In 1997, Glenn decided that he wanted to leave advertising to join what would become the first of three Internet start-ups he got involved in. The challenge appealed to him, and the risk: He needed to find a new edge, and he was ready to give up steady income to pursue a big upside. Meg wasn't thrilled with the idea—she has been risk averse her entire life. But the two of them negotiated, and six months after Glenn began his new job, Meg left hers to return to real estate finance. The two of them had built up a considerable overhead, and by working 70 hours a week, 52 weeks a year—common hours for the highly competitive, upper-end New York market she was working in—Meg figured the family wouldn't have to sacrifice its standard of living while Glenn was going for the gold. Thanks to the cell phone and laptop, Glenn also could work partially out of the home and keep an eye on their now three children.

The problem came after the third of Glenn's Internet start-ups fell victim to the Nasdaq collapse. Of the three, one had proved a financial success. Simultaneously, Meg was running into her own wall at work. "I became mean and testy," she says. When she looked inside herself, Meg knew the gig was up. She walked into her boss's office and told him so, and the two of them worked out a new schedule that allowed her more flexible hours.

Now, she and Glenn are negotiating again. He has gone back to steady work, at AOL Time Warner as director of business development, and a regular income. She's thinking about striking out on her own, not a big-risk operation—that's not part of her fundamental work personality—but something that will free up her time and help her find more creativity in her life. It's Meg's season to reinvent, Glenn's to hunker down and allow it to happen. I asked Meg if the tense moments and many choices they had lived through had ever threatened their relationship.

"Not really," she told me. "We take the long view. There's time for each of us to get what we want, just not all at once or at the very same moment all the time. We have a kind of old-fashioned view," which is not really old-fashioned at all.

The last time I saw Meg, she told me that they were talking about selling their place in the city and moving to something much more like the small farm she had grown up on, a way to transform their physical assets into the energy that can fuel a more entrepreneurial period for them both. For right now, she said, it's a form of play for them, but it's play with a deadly serious purpose.

"We create these multiple futures, try them on, and then decide which one to step into," Meg explained. "We can get very mad at each other in this process—there's a lot at stake—but then we get the outline of our next chapter and come back together, and everything's cool again."

When I think of Glenn and Meg, I imagine one of those incredibly complicated tribal dances where first one partner, then the other, steps forward to claim the lead while the other retreats to the background to begin summoning new spirits. In essence, they are using their coupleship to manage the dual risk of serial living. Loretta LaRoche puts me more in mind of a solitary wilderness trek—she has gone through hard times, many of them alone. But one of the beauties of this way of living is that it comes out to the same place in the end, however you get there: Reinvention unlocks possibility.

Loretta grew up in an extended Italian family, supported by her mother, who worked as a secretary. She was married by her junior year in college, and a mother herself by graduation. For 10 years, she filled the role of supermom, cooking for the family and making sure the kids got to their schools and games. Then, early in the 1970s, she was divorced and ended up basically with nothing—no work experience, no money, with three children at home who needed her. Welfare and food stamps helped bridge the gap. So did a job waiting tables 12 to 15 hours a day at Friendly's. Finally, she got hired by a spa chain to run an exercise class. For Loretta, it was her first "real" job, and she meant to succeed at it. She had an idea— radical for the time—that combining exercise with music would result in an enjoyable workout that was more aerobically sound than the standard grunt and groan. The spa chain, though, wasn't having anything to do with it.

Fired, still out of money and with no car, Loretta used her last $450 to rent a small studio space for her own exercise program and invited 75 of the women she had known at the spa to take part. As the program caught on—she was teaching up to six classes a day by herself—Loretta began to notice that while many of her clients were feeling better physically, whatever emotional problems had led them to her classes weren't being addressed. It was the inner dialogue, not the absence of muscle tone, that was causing their problems. Soon, she was reading up on mental health and studying cognitive therapy, and from that developed one of the earliest exercise programs stressing the mind-body connection.

In the same spirit, Loretta became interested in therapeutic touch and began offering a one-day program for nurses on touch and healing. That, in turn, caught the eye of a PBS producer who, after four years of back and forth, finally managed to attach a five-minute segment on her work to the end of another documentary. From that developed a video, *The Joy of Stress*, that sold 100,000 copies. Loretta, it turned out, had a comedian's natural sense of timing as well as a firm belief that laughter can heal. The video brought her to the attention of Harvard's Mind-Body Medical Institute, where she would spend 10 years working with patients and developing the Humor and Optimism Program. In 1989, she published her first book: *Relax, You May Only Have a Few Minutes Left*. Now in her sixties, Loretta speaks all over the country and has just finished a second book.

Were you at all tempted, I asked Loretta, to take just any job during the time when you were out of money and trying to get the exercise studio off the ground? "You know," she said, "I looked at other jobs, but I got physically ill every time I did." I had been there, too.

Comfortable, this life is not. Nor especially convenient. There's risk and there's fear in serial living, but what we get at the end is, I think, the most valuable thing any of us can own: freedom, freedom to be what we can be and what we want to be, freedom to grow and to follow our desires and to make our dreams come true, freedom to pursue a future that is waiting for each of us alone, freedom to succeed, freedom to fail, freedom to create a life that like the greatest works of art is a constant process of becoming.

Resources

For further information on *Chapters* and the related areas below, visit *www.TransitionsInstitute.net*:

- One-day seminar on the principles of living successfully in chapters

- One-on-one Navigator consultations

- Training program for company founders/boards

- Center for Executive Options: high-end transitions and venture services for CEOs

- Navigator Program for company founders/boards

Or e-mail the author at *Chaptersthebook@aol.com*

To enlist the services of the Transition Coaches referred to in this book, call (212) 628-1169 and provide your contact information:

Transitions Institute
David Zelman, Ph.D.

Center for Executive Options
Phil Simhauser

To further reference the works of the authors mentioned:

William Bridges, *Transitions: Making Sense of Life's Changes*, Perseus Press, New York, 1980; originally published by Addison-Wesley Publishing Co. Inc., Reading, Massachusetts.

Deepak Chopra, *The Seven Spiritual Laws of Success*, Amber-Allen Publishing, San Rafael, California, 1995.

Stephen Covey, *Seven Habits of Highly Successful People*, Fireside—Simon & Schuster, New York, 1990.

Robert Fritz, *Creating*, Fawcett Books, New York, 1993.

Ellen Galinksy, Families and Work Institute, *www.familiesandwork.com*.

Carole Hyatt and Linda Gottlieb, *When Smart People Fail: Rebuilding Yourself for Success*, Penguin USA, New York, 1993; originally published by Simon & Schuster, New York, 1987.

Rosabeth Moss Kanter, *Evolve!: Succeeding in the Digital Culture of Tomorrow*, Harvard Business School Press, Boston, Massachusetts, 2001.

Donald Marrs, *Executive in Passage*, Barrington Sky Publishing, Los Angeles, California, 1990. (To order call 800-729-0129.)

John O'Neil, *The Paradox of Success*, Tarcher Penguin Putnam Inc., New York, 1993.

Yankelovich Partners, "Rocking the Ages: A Study," *www.yankelovich.com*.

Credits

About the Author

Candice Carpenter cofounded iVillage, the leading online network for women, in 1995, served as its CEO for the company's first five years and chairman of the board for six. Before launching iVillage, she ran emerging businesses at American Express, QVC, and Time Warner. She is now a wife, mother, author, speaker, and managing director of the Transitions Institute. She is a winner of the Matrix Award, the highest peer award for women in media; the Award for Entrepreneurial Leadership from MIT; and an Emmy for prime-time television.

In her twenties, Ms. Carpenter was one of America's premier female mountaineers. She holds a BA from Stanford and an MBA from Harvard Business School. Over the past several years, Carpenter has been a featured speaker at Harvard, Radcliff, Stanford, MIT, the London School of Economics, and the Davos World Economic Forum, as well as the Gartner Group, Goldman Sachs, PaineWebber, the BusinessWeek CEO Conference, Fast Company Conferences, and the Committee of 200.